ReOrganize Your Life™

True Meaning To The Power Of Organizing

Ray Anthony Poole

Copyright © 2006 by Ray Anthony Poole

ReOrganize Your Life
by Ray Anthony Poole

Printed in the United States of America

ISBN 1-60034-184-5
Library of Congress Control Number: 2006901474

All rights reserved solely by the author. The author guarantees all contents are original and do not infringe upon the legal rights of any other person or work. No part of this book may be reproduced in any form without the permission of the author. The views expressed in this book are not necessarily those of the publisher.

Unless otherwise designated, Scripture quotations are taken from the King James Version Bible.

References marked AMP; Scripture quotations taken from the Amplified® Bible, Copyright © 1954, 1958, 1962, 1964, 1965, 1987 by The Lockman Foundation. Used by permission. (www.Lockman.org)

Scripture references marked ASV are taken from the Holy Bible American Standard Version; Copyright © 1901; Star Bible Publications, Inc, Fort Worth, TX.

Scripture quotations marked (ESV) are from The Holy Bible, English Standard Version, copyright © 2001 by Crossway Bibles, a division of Good News Publishers. Used by permission. All rights reserved.

www.xulonpress.com

ReOrganize Your Life ™
ROYL ™
ROYL Principles ™

15333 Culver Drive
Suite 340-434
Irvine, California 92604
www.ReOrganizeYourLife.com

Dedication

To GOD be all The Glory; JESUS CHRIST, LORD and SAVIOUR and The HOLY SPIRIT, without you I am nothing I am to be. Thank you.

My wife, Dena Olivia—my love, my help, my good thing and favor of the LORD. *(Whoso findeth a wife findeth a good thing, and obtaineth favour of the LORD. Proverb 18:22.) (The heart of her husband doth safely trust in her, so that he shall have no need of spoil. Proverb 31:11)*

My son, Ray Jr, his wife, Jennifer and their sons, (my grandsons), Joshua and Isaiah—a heritage and blessing from GOD, my unceasing love. *(Children's children are the crown of old men; and the glory of children are their fathers. Proverb 17:6).*

My daughter, Brittany Dene—my love always, unconditionally.— *(Many daughters have done virtuously, but thou excellest them all. Proverb 31:29.)*

My father, Benny; my mother, Barbara (whom I will always love and honor) and my sisters and brothers—the natural genesis and affections of my life. *(Thy father and thy mother shall be glad, and she that bare thee shall rejoice. Proverb 23:25)*; Sharon, Teresa, Benny Jr., Janice, Rodney; Jean and Laila *(Be kindly affectioned one to another with brotherly love; in honour preferring one another; Romans 12:10)*

My mother in law, Anna Parker; your support and giving heart is truly a blessing from the LORD. —*(Blessed are the pure in heart: for they shall see God. Matthew 5:8)*

Acknowledgements

"Iron sharpeneth iron; so a man sharpeneth the countenance of his friend." Proverb 27:17

Michael and Sabrina Todd—more than friends; Sabrina, thank you for your editing skills on this Book; I appreciate both of you.

David Kositchek and the Staff of Kositchek's, Lansing MI.—my respect; thanks for allowing me those precious days of friendship and fellowship and, of course, the fine attire. Mansfield Joseph Morris, I will always remember you and our many conversations.

The late, W. James (Jim) Russell—Mentor, encourager, friend and wise counsel.—*Matthew 29:19-20*

Doug and Cathy Wray—real friends love at all times (Proverb 17:17), thanks.

Mr. Billy W. Norris & Jamie Jones—perpetual friends from the days of high school.

Arthur Andrews—a man of true friendship, as the many years are a witness.

Brett and Wendy Walker & family—heartfelt friends
Stan and Karen Sims—faithful friends
Bill and Diane Burton—sincere friends
Suki Bur—a genuine friend

Patty Williams and Staff of Beaner's Gourmet Coffee®, Okemos, MI

Dave and Tina Martinez and Staff of It's A Grind Coffee House®, Irvine, CA

The "24/IAG" Friends—thanks for allowing me to be a part of the crew; Dan, Moss, John, Nelson, Frank, Mychele, Barbara, Chuck, Shannon, Inniss, Fred, and Jay

La familia de amigos—Anthony M, Eric S., Eric W., Claudia O., Monica M., Hilda D., Kim S., Anita M., Maria R., Maria C., Arlene R., Cheryl R., Alma H, Susan G., John R., Adam, Andrew Natividad and JR Hendricks (Hugo R. & Gilbert P.)

Special Acknowledgement:

Pastors, Drs. James and Stacia Pierce and Life Changers Christian Center—thank you, for allowing GOD to use you.

Joshua Prizer, 123 PrintFinder for Logo completion

To GOD alone be the glory

Empero hagáse todo decentemente y con orden.

Let all things be done decently and in order.
(1Corinthians 14:40 KJV)

But all things should be done with regard to decency and propriety and in an orderly fashion.
(1Corinthians 14:40 AMP)

All things in life should be done honestly and in an organized manner.
Ray Anthony Poole

Praise be to GOD

Contents

About The Author xiii

Preface xv

CHAPTER ONE 17
It's Time To ReOrganize Your Life, Now! 19

CHAPTER TWO 33
What Do You Mean ReOrganize? 35

CHAPTER THREE 53
What Areas Do I ReOrganize? 55

CHAPTER FOUR 91
The Essentials For ReOrganizing 93

CHAPTER FIVE 113
Easy Steps To Stay ReOrganized 115

CHAPTER SIX 127
True Meaning To The Power Of Organizing 129

CHAPTER SEVEN 157
ROYL For CHRIST 159

Endnotes..175

About the Author

Ray Anthony Poole was an Associate Pastor, administrator and member of a church in Lansing Michigan for ten and a half years, where he had responsibility for the general function and order of church services, overseer of twenty departments, Dean of Ministers in Training and along with his wife Dena, had responsibility for the Married Couples Ministry. With a Bachelors of Science Degree in Psychology and Sociology, he has over twenty-nine years of management, administration and organization experience with the government of the State of Michigan, before retiring. He and his wife currently live in Irvine, California. Mr. Poole is recognized as an authority in ReOrganizing.

Born in Jackson, Michigan and moving to the Lansing area soon after graduating from university, Mr. Poole began an interesting career with the State of Michigan; employed as a correctional officer, psychometrist, assistant human resource director and administrator.

Mr. Poole was ordained as a minister in 1994 and has three great life objectives; to shine and glorify GOD, to be a good and faithful servant and to go minister, by preaching and publishing the Word of GOD; helping to build up the Church, the people of GOD.

Having a passion for the Word of GOD, he enjoys reading and studying the Bible and desires to teach and share the great wisdom and principles of life found within the Scriptures.

Preface

When it comes to organizing you, probably as most people, will primarily focus on household and office clutter. Thus, most of your valuable time and effort in life will be toward developing various purging and simplified storage solutions, while forgetting about the "big picture" of your life.

According to the *Organizing Resources Statistics* (Organizing Resources.com), research has shown that a significant number of individuals believe that "the number one irritant of American homes is clutter" and "experts say that 80% of household congestion…is the result of disorganization rather than insufficient space".

While these statistics may be true, I believe that to effectively deal with the "clutter" in a more comprehensive manner, you must have a broader view of ReOrganizing Your Life™. To sustain any improvements gained by the "purge and storage" method of handling the household clutter you must, also, deal with the other critical areas of your life, such as; what you believe (doctrine), relationships, resources and time.

ReOrganize Your Life™ is a treatise on how to organize your total life, using the wisdom of the Scriptures.

"Every Scripture is God-breathed (given by His inspiration) and profitable for instruction, for reproof {and} conviction

of sin, for correction of error {and} discipline in obedience, [and] for training in righteousness (in holy living, in conformity to God's will in thought, purpose, and action),"
"So that the man of God may be complete {and} proficient, well fitted {and} thoroughly equipped for every good work."
2 Timothy 3:16-17 AMP

Taking the time to ReOrganize Your Life™ now will be extremely profitable for your future. I sincerely believe that each area of your life can be ReOrganized by following the ways of GOD, as given by HIS inspiration and common everyday practices.

The general purpose of this Book is to; 1.) be a source for teaching how to ReOrganize, 2.) be a source for biblical application for living, 3.) be a source for reading verses of the Bible and 4.) be a source for initiating study of the Bible.

While using just a few personal examples from my life, my intention is to give the reader strong biblical examples and principles as it relates to ReOrganizing Your Life.

If you are ready for real change in your life, then go ahead and begin to ReOrganize Your Life™, now! "Go get it, simply go get it".

CHAPTER ONE

It's Time To ReOrganize Your Life, Now!

For though I be absent in the flesh, yet am I with you in the spirit, joying and *beholding your order*, and the stedfastness of your faith in Christ. Colossians 2:5 {Emphasis added}

CHAPTER ONE

It's Time To ReOrganize Your Life, Now!

The Bible says to *"Let all things be done decently and in order."* (1Corinthians 14:40) This scripture verse happens to be one of the structural building blocks for maintaining balance in my life.

I believe that GOD created everything to happen in, and to be in, an organized or orderly fashion. The Amplified Bible for 1 Corinthians 14:40 reads: *"But all things should be done with regard to decency and propriety and in an orderly fashion"*

"Good order is the foundation of all good things." [1]

For a person who strives to maintain order in their life as the scripture suggests, (and as I put it), "all things *should* be done honestly and in an organized manner".

We see order each and every day of our lives. Even when we may not recognize it, order exists in our "normal" routines, as we function daily in life. As a matter of fact, what we call our normal routine is essentially a form of established order created by us as a seemingly simplified means of living.

Whether by design or unintended default, we have organized our lives to be what it is today. In an attempt to maintain stability we have allowed, mostly by default, an established way of ordering our lives.

It is now time to take a look and behold the various areas of our life, its routines and surroundings, in order to see what we have created. It's time to ReOrganize Your Life™, now!

Although people may not see you or be in your presence at the time, the extent of order in your life is still apparent.

> *"For though I be absent in the flesh, yet am I with you in the spirit, joying and **beholding your order**, and the stedfastness of your faith in Christ." Colossians 2:5 (Emphasis added)*

People with whom you have a relationship can see (behold) if your life is in good order. Having a well-regulated life, a life properly ordered, is important. A life of instability, chaos or confusion lacks proper order; "in a world of chaos, most people crave order" [2].

You Must Make The Decision To Change

"Know that it's your decisions, not your conditions, that determine your destiny" — Anonymous.

Making the decision to change may be one of the most important things you do that can have extraordinary results for your future.

You must make the decision to change and ReOrganize Your Life™ (ROYL™). It's time to ReOrganize Your Life™ for change. ROYL is pronounced royal.

According to dictionaries, *change* commonly means; to put or take something in place of something else, substitute for, replace with, to cause to become different, transform, convert, undergo alteration or replacement.

In short, the implication is that to change at one point in time for an individual, may mean to completely replace something. At some other point in time or in some other area of one's life, change may mean to alter something.

The decision to ReOrganize Your Life™ (ROYL™) is about managing or ordering your life. Life management is at the very core or root of life itself. An individual that does not take the time to change and reorganize their life is on a road toward increased confusion, chaos and destruction. This is especially true in the 21st Century, with change happening at "the speed of light".

The case for change and reorganizing can be seen by numerous natural examples, which witness to us that our lives are changing. Our lives continue to be impacted drastically each and every minute, as a result of the Technological-Information Age in which we currently find ourselves. With the achievements in technology and the capability to send information instantly anywhere in the world, we literally do see change happening at the speed of light.

"The shift from an Industrial to an Information Society is bound to be breathtaking. The transition from one stage of economic life to another has always involved a revolution. We think that the Information Revolution is likely to be the most far-reaching of all. It will reorganize life more thoroughly than either the Agricultural Revolution or the Industrial Revolution. And its impact will be felt in a fraction of the time" [3].

The need to change and to ReOrganize Your Life™ (ROYL™) is crucial, if not critical for most people in the world today. ROYL™ is a key factor in the 21st Century for growth or success in every area of life. Your future growth or success depends upon order, but you must begin to transition towards managing your life, by first reorganizing your life.

"We live in a period of PROFOUND TRANSITION—and the changes are more radical perhaps than even those that ushered in the "Second Industrial Revolution" of the middle of the 19th century, or the structural changes triggered by the Great Depression and the Second World War" [4].

Each person's life is in need of proper order. The proper order depends upon the season, the time and the situation or circumstances surrounding one's life. Thus, it is vitally important to understand what order is all about, how you go about establishing order and what is the proper order for your life.

We can see (behold) that order is at the very center or core of everything that GOD has done and does in all creation.

ReOrganize Your Life

In the beginning of mankind, GOD, the Great ReOrganizer, first established or set forth order; as witnessed by the first chapter of the book of Genesis. GOD started mankind by reorganizing life.

The Bible is the book to use for beginning to ReOrganize Your Life™. Within the first five books of the Holy Bible, Almighty GOD, through the patriarch Moses, lays out the most extensive, collective, and personal plan to ReOrganize Your Life™.

The Pentateuch, which means Law, is the first five books of the Bible and establishes certain laws of order (or organization) to life for mankind. Sometimes there is a need to change; depending upon the internal or external factors surrounding one's life.

- Genesis signifies *a beginning.*
- Exodus signifies *a departure or going out.*
- Leviticus signifies *an establishment of rules and methods or observances.*
- Numbers signifies *a counting, inventory, or sorting.*
- Deuteronomy signifies *a repetition of the law or a reordering.*

It should be evident in our life that, there is a *beginning*, when we recognize things are chaotic and may be out of balance. Then, there may be an urging to *depart or go out* from the chaos and imbalance, which surrounds us.

Further, we begin to understand that the chaos or imbalance may be the result of not adhering to certain *established rules, methods or observances*. This may lead us to begin to *count, inventory, or sort* and take note of matters. Finally, we may understand the simple need for a *repetition of certain laws or a reordering* of matters. Essentially, it is the understanding of the need for you to change and ReOrganize Your Life™.

We must recognize that things are always changing around us, whether we want them to or not. It is a fact that, if you do not change some things on your own in your life, certain things will be changed any way. We must begin to use wisdom, knowledge and understanding to change those things we have some control over. Daniel, of the Bible, said that GOD changes things and gives wisdom and knowledge to them that know understanding.

Daniel answered and said, Blessed be the name of God for ever and ever: for wisdom and might are his: And he changeth the times and the seasons: he removeth kings, and setteth up kings: he giveth wisdom unto the wise, and knowledge to them that know understanding: Daniel 2:20-21

GOD changes the times and the seasons to order one's life according to His wisdom and might.

GOD does not, only, change the times and seasons; He removes and sets up leaders and gives wisdom and knowledge to those who get understanding. (Proverbs 4:7; James 1:5)

In addition, we as Christians are constantly being changed (or should be) by the Word of GOD as we allow the Spirit of the LORD to change us.

Now the Lord is that Spirit: and where the Spirit of the Lord is, there is liberty. But we all, with open face beholding as in a glass the glory of the Lord, are changed into the same image from glory to glory, even as by the Spirit of the Lord. 2 Corinthians 3:17-18

It must be time to ReOrganize Your Life™! Say to your self, "It's time to ReOrganize my life!" Please, say it again, "It's time to ReOrganize my life!"

As we grow, and in order to grow, we must constantly reorganize certain areas in our life. You must ReOrganize Your Life™! When you ReOrganize Your Life, you will actually begin to simplify and add balance to your life.

You may need to ReOrganize Your Life™ (ROYL™) to bring back a proper balance to your life. Maintaining a proper life balance is possible through ROYL™. Life balance is important for maintaining the necessary personal perspective on a daily or regular basis.

As indicated earlier, your life already has some order, whether good or bad, now you need to ReOrganize Your Life™ to change certain areas or ways. We must reorganize our life because we may have started to build upon the right foundation, but we did not always adhere to the original blueprint for laying the foundation. Thus you must continually look at the need to ReOrganize Your Life™.

"According to the grace of God which is given unto me, as a wise masterbuilder, I have laid the foundation, and another buildeth thereon. But let every man take heed how he buildeth thereupon. For other foundation can no man lay than that is laid, which is Jesus Christ." 1Corinthians 3:10-11

In the beginning, GOD created the heaven and the earth. The earth was unformed, void and dark. Genesis chapters one and two of the Bible are foundation chapters of GOD's divine reorganization of the earth and life on the earth.

I believe that, within these two chapters, GOD gave mankind foundation principles on how to reorganize anything on the earth, thus letting all things to be done decently and in order. More of this will be discussed in Chapter 6, of this book.

We must also realize that, the need to ReOrganize Your Life™ is a life-long process. When we finish reorganizing our life there will be a need to examine the area or ways on a regular basis, in the future, in order to maintain the accomplishment.

It is clear in the Bible that GOD has given each of us an expected end.

For I know the thoughts that I think toward you, saith the LORD, thoughts of peace, and not of evil, to give you an expected end. Jeremiah 29:11

Even though GOD's thoughts towards us is to give us an expected end or outcome in life; certain situations, circumstances, events or other things impact our lives and begin to get us off focus, off track or disorganized at times, from the expected end.

This is why we must realize that the need to ReOrganize Your Life™ is a life-long process. So we must constantly reorganize our life, when necessary, to stay on focus or on the course to God's expected end for our life.

One of my greatest natural amazement and joy in life is flying. The wonder of combining natural laws and the technological dynamics of flying an aircraft is truly amazing to me. Of the reasons that flying an aircraft is exciting to me is the tremendous amount of organization that it takes to fly the aircraft to its expected destination.

As a matter of fact, organization is at the very core of the flying experience. The pilot is responsible for each detail of the aircraft, which means that the physical condition, function and coordination of the various instruments must be in proper working order before attempting takeoff.

The organized manner in which flying the aircraft takes place is very precise and orderly. In general, the process of flying includes taxi, takeoff, climbing, cruising, descent, approach and landing. Each of the separate areas in the process has its own organized method and checklist for accomplishing the expected end.

A jet plane has an autopilot function, an automatic guidance system, which allows the jet to fly automatically by programming certain information to assist in reaching the expected destination.

Although the aircraft is set on autopilot, the pilot must still constantly monitor the instruments to be assured of staying on course, even with the autopilot activated. This is because certain conditions may affect the pre-programmed course and may get the aircraft off course. An aircraft may get off course by a few degrees, which will affect the expected end or which could even be fatal.

Most people set the "autopilot of life" on, and do not look to see if they are still on the course that GOD pre-programmed, that expected end.

Some of us have our "autopilot of life" on constantly and we are still off course of where GOD wants us to be at this point in time.

Because of our automatic guidance system, some of us may be off course a few degrees, which could be affecting the quality of life we are currently living. Some of us may be off course 180 degrees and going in the complete opposite direction of our expected end.

So then, you may ask yourself what I must do to get back on course in my life. How do I turn around and go in the direction of my expected end?

You Must Take Immediate ReOrganized Action

To ReOrganize Your Life™, you must take immediate reorganized action.

> *"Talk no more so very proudly; let not arrogance go forth from your mouth, for the Lord is a God of <u>knowledge</u>, and by Him <u>actions</u> are weighed." 1Samuel 2:3 AMP [emphasis added]*

GOD is a God of knowledge and thus desires His children to seek knowledge like Him, as a father. GOD is also, a God of action and weighs (balances or measures) the action according to His desires he gives us.

"Talk is cheap" was a saying as I was growing up. Most people can talk about taking action, but their pride or arrogance outweighs anything coming from their mouth and hinders any real or concrete action.

Once you have made the decision to change, next you must take immediate reorganized action to ReOrganize Your Life. *Realize and believe that you are the only one who controls your future.*

Taking immediate reorganized action means that you must begin to obtain the proper knowledge related to the area in your life. In other words, you must know what you want to do or what you ought to do.

"Knowing and doing are inseparable elements in the pursuit and accomplishment of worthy goals. Knowledge by itself is passive and ineffective. Action driven by vain ambition without sufficient knowledge will invariably be unproductive and even destructive. Desired results, then are produced only in a marriage of appropriate knowledge with organized action". [5]

I like to say that, desired results are produced only in a marriage of appropriate knowledge with reorganized action. That is, get the appropriate knowledge, and then start to reorganize what you are currently doing in your life.

You are already on your way to taking immediate reorganized action, simply by reading this book. You are now getting the necessary general knowledge that will help you obtain the desired results to ReOrganize Your Life™.

"The heart of the prudent getteth knowledge; and the ear of the wise seeketh knowledge." Proverb 18:15

Getting the knowledge that you need and the wisdom to do whatever it is that you wish to do is the primary and immediate action needed towards reorganizing.

In addition, you may need to seek other materials in order to assist with the pursuit of the action, such as the Bible, and informational or instructional publications; books, magazines, the Internet, CD's or tapes. It is also recommended that you consider talking to individuals who may be subject matter experts or have wisdom in a particular area.

Knowledge is just information or data, until it is organized. To be helpful and to accomplish a desire or goal, knowledge must be organized.

I remember that, while living in Jackson, Michigan (my hometown), after graduating from Central Michigan University (Mt. Pleasant, Michigan) in the summer of 1973, I decided to fulfill a desire I had of going to California, with the idea of living there for awhile. I know, this was not a unique venture, especially during this time, but it was something that I strongly desired to do.

Months prior to this time, I told close friends of my desire to "stake my claim in the Golden State" but not many believed that I was serious and even in certain ways indirectly discouraged the notion. One friend at the time, however, had hope in the idea, mainly because of his desire to go to California and little means to get there. So, I cannot truly say that he even believed me.

One lesson I learned from this experience was that; sometimes talking about your desire with others or discussing actions that you want to take, may not be a great idea until you have an organized action plan. And then, you should be strategic with whom you share certain plans.

Determined not to let others discourage me from my decision towards accomplishing my desire, I took *immediate reorganized action*, by getting my plan together. Part of the plan was to get the knowledge needed to complete the journey.

I began to read as much as I could about California. I began to put some money away for the trip. I obtained maps of California and various routes for driving across the USA. I determined the month, week, day and time that I would leave.

Next, I had to decide what of my earthly possessions of value I would take with me. (Actually this was probably the easiest of the things to decide since I hadn't accumulated many material things). As the day and time approached I informed the one friend mentioned earlier that I was leaving, packed my car, filled the gas tank up and began to fulfill the journey of my long awaited desire.

In actuality, the journey began when I made *the decision to change* and took *immediate reorganized action*. Getting the knowledge and taking the simple steps towards that desire of going to California, did not only complete my goal, it was also the beginning of some important changes in my life.

By *making the decision to change* and taking *immediate reorganized action* in this one area opened the door for more significant changes in the character of my life.

Through this condensed version of accomplishing my vision of going to California, you can get a good, but simple, idea of what may be involved and how you may use the steps to ReOrganize Your Life™.

What is so good about taking action is that you should be ready to see the greater impact it can have in other areas of your life later.

Sometimes you just need to step out in faith on your ideas and reoccurring thoughts, or desires locked up in your heart. Your ideas are searching for a means of expression. GOD gives us the desires of our heart, to accomplish His purpose for us.

No matter how small the desire, it just may be the initial step towards that greater desire or some major change on the horizon. It may begin with the desire to reorganize your closet, the kitchen cabinets, the garage, basement, the bookshelf, the office or some other area of your life.

The main point is, to *"go get it; simply, go get it"*. Make the decision to change and take immediate reorganized action! It's up to you; don't put it off for tomorrow. You do not know what tomorrow may bring. Suki Bur, a friend and former co-worker would always remind those of us around her that, "life's too short!"

> *"Come now, you who say, Today or tomorrow we will go into such and such a city and spend a year there and carry on our business and make money." "Yet you do not know [the least thing] about what may happen tomorrow. What is the nature of your life? You are [really] but a wisp of vapor (a puff of smoke, a mist) that is visible for a little while and then disappears [into thin air]." "You ought instead to say, If the Lord is willing, we shall live and we shall do this or that [thing]." James 4:13-15*

It's time to ReOrganize Your Life™ by beginning to make certain and definite changes in your life.

Decision + Knowledge + ReOrganized Action = Change

CHAPTER ONE

ROYL Principles ™

Seven ROYL Principles:

1. To ReOrganize Your Life, all things *should* be done honestly and in an organized manner.

2. To ReOrganize Your Life, make the decision to change.

3. To ReOrganize Your Life, the Bible is the book to use for beginning.

4. To ReOrganize Your Life, realize that, the need is a life-long process.

5. To ReOrganize Your Life, take immediate reorganized action.

6. To ReOrganize Your Life, begin to obtain the proper knowledge.

7. To ReOrganize Your Life, *"Go get it; simply, go get it"*.

CHAPTER TWO

What Do You Mean, ReOrganize?

Whoso offereth praise glorifieth me: and to him that *ordereth his conversation aright* will I shew the *salvation* of God. Psalm 50:23 {Emphasis added}

CHAPTER TWO

What Do You Mean, ReOrganize?

When we reorganize areas of our life, we begin the process of simplifying our life. Remember, in the previous chapter, we said to *"Let all things be done decently and in order." 1 Corinthians 14:40*

Defining the Words

Well, for this chapter, let us begin in order by defining the words "re", "order", "organize" and "reorganize". According to the dictionaries, the most common definitions for each of the words are as follows:

<u>Re</u>: means again, anew, over again.

<u>Order</u>: means the sequence or arrangement of things or events; a fixed or definite plan; law of arrangement; an established method or system; **organize**.

<u>Organize</u>: means to provide with an organic structure; to arrange in an orderly way; to make into a whole with unified and coherent relationships; to make plans or arrange for; to

*bring into being; to establish; to set (one self) into an orderly state of mind; to gather available elements or resources into a functional arrangement; {synonyms: **order**, arrange, systemize, formulate, develop, create, bring together, and establish}.*

<u>*Reorganize*</u>*: to organize again or anew; to place in order again; return to order; to arrange again; to bring order to again or anew.*

Based upon the above, we could read verse forty of First Corinthians chapter fourteen this way; *Let all things be done decently and **<u>organized</u>***.

Again, as previously stated in Chapter One of this book, the Amplified Bible for *1 Corinthians 14:40* reads, *"But all things should be done with regard to decency and propriety and in an orderly fashion."* In other words, we could also say that, *all things should be done honorably or honestly (decently) and in proper order or in an organized way.*

As we begin to reorganize our lives we actually are in preparation for future demonstrations of the blessings of GOD, in the form of tangible results. In other words, when we put things in their proper order, opportunities in our lives begin to open up for us.

When we reorganize and have order in our lives, we can obtain liberty or a real since of freedom. We are delivered from chaos and confusion, we begin to allow prosperity in each area of our life and we place ourselves in a position of safety.

To further explain, and as an additional example of the expectation of order or being organized in our lives, let's turn to Psalm chapter fifty verse twenty-three. First reading from the Amplified Bible:

"He who brings an offering of praise and thanksgiving honors and glorifies Me; and he who orders his way aright [who prepares the way that I may show him], to him I will demonstrate the salvation of God" Psalm 50:23 (AMP)

And the King James Version;

"Whoso offereth praise glorifieth me: and to him that ordereth his conversation aright will I shew the salvation of God" Psalm 50:23 (KJV)

Now let's get an understanding of what we've just read, in relation to organizing, by studying or analyzing a few words in this particular verse.

First, that word <u>ordereth</u> [6] (in Hebrew, sum or sim, Strong's #7760) means to put, to set; establish; to erect; to plant; to make; to constitute; to appoint; to turn; to change; to put something somewhere. The word ordereth by implication means to organize.

Next, the word; <u>conversation</u> [7] (in Hebrew, derek or derekh, Strong's #7760) means a going; walk; journey; way; path; road; mode; manner; course; way of life. The word conversation refers to a course or mode of actions and behaviors in life; in other words, your way of life.

The word; <u>aright</u> simply means properly or correctly.

And now the word; <u>salvation</u> (in the Hebrew, yesha) means liberty, deliverance, prosperity and safety.

Therefore, *Psalm 50:23* could read: Whoever offers praise, glorifies GOD: and to him that organizes (*ordereth*) his way of life (*conversation*) properly (*aright*) will GOD show the liberty, deliverance, prosperity and safety (*salvation*) of GOD.

Or, Whoever offers praise, glorifies GOD: and to him that organizes his way of life properly will GOD show the liberty, deliverance, prosperity and safety of GOD.

GOD is interested in us organizing our life properly.

But seek ye first the kingdom of God, and his righteousness; and all these things shall be added unto you. Matthew 6:33

Properly organizing your life means that you must ReOrganize Your Life™ and put GOD first. We need to reorganize our ways in life, so that GOD can show us His salvation, opportunities of liberty, deliverance, prosperity and safety.

Say this; "I'm beginning to see that I may need to reorganize my life!" ReOrganize Your Life™ for opportunities of liberty, deliverance, prosperity and safety.

Now Consider Your Ways

To ReOrganize Your Life™, means that you must now consider your ways. That is, you must look at who you are and how you do the things you do. You must now consider <u>your</u> ways, not the ways of your neighbors, not the ways of your relatives, not the ways of your co-workers, not the ways of your boss, not the ways of your pastor, not the ways of your friends, but now consider <u>your</u> ways!

You need to understand you, and the ways that you do things. It's time now, to consider your ways.

Turning to the Bible in *Haggai Chapter1 verses 1 through 8,* we encounter the word of the LORD, essentially saying, by the prophet Haggai, "**Now...Consider your ways.**" We see here, an appeal to rebuild the temple at a specific time (now, which was in the second year of Darius the king, in the sixth month, in the first day of the month).

In the story of Haggai; Haggai, is exhorting or encouraging the people to organize and take action to rebuild the temple of GOD which was destroyed previously. We see that, this was the specific time to begin. We must also, discern and recognize the specific time to reorganize or rebuild upon certain areas in our life.

It came time to rebuild, even though the people had not yet recognized that it was time to rebuild. Sometimes we may not yet see it, but this may now be the specific season and time to begin reorganizing your life.

"In the second year of Darius the king, in the sixth month, in the first day of the month, came the word of the Lord by

Haggai the prophet unto Zerubbabel the son of Shealtiel, governor of Judah, and to Joshua the son of Josedech, the high priest, saying,"

"Thus speaketh the Lord of hosts, saying, This people say, The time is not come, the time that the Lord's house should be built."

"Then came the word of the Lord by Haggai the prophet, saying,"

"Is it time for you, o ye, to dwell in your cieled houses, and this house lie waste?"

*"**Now** therefore thus saith the Lord of hosts; **Consider your ways**."*

"Ye have sown much, and bring in little; ye eat, but ye have not enough; ye drink, but ye are not filled with drink; ye clothe you, but there is none warm; and he that earneth wages earneth wages to put it into a bag with holes."

*"Thus saith the Lord of hosts; **Consider your ways**."*

"Go up to the mountain, and bring wood, and build the house; and I will take pleasure in it, and I will be glorified, saith the Lord." [Emphasis added]

It's time now, to consider your ways before you "go up to the mountain, and bring wood, and build…"

A Characteristic of Disorganization

Before we further discuss considering your ways, we must first point out some characteristics of disorganization or disorder. When there is disorganization you will have or see waste. In Haggai 1 verse

4, it says, *"Is it time for you, o ye, to dwell in your cieled houses, and this house lie **waste**?"*

The word waste is the Hebrew word *charev {Strong's #2720}*, which means: dry, parched, ruined or desolate. [8]

As we can also see, in Verse 6, the description is of waste; dryness, being parched, ruined, or desolate; which is that you do a lot (you sow a lot), there is plenty of activity, but there is little order to show for it. In other words, there is much action but it is wasted, as placing money into a bag with holes.

> *"Ye have sown much, and bring in little; ye eat, but ye have not enough; ye drink, but ye are not filled with drink; ye clothe you, but there is none warm; and he that earneth wages earneth wages to put it into a bag with holes." Haggai 1:6*

Where there is disorganization or disorder, you will often have or see some form of waste.

It may be a sign of waste of time, which is, not using time efficiently or effectively. It may be a sign of waste in not utilizing space effectively. It may be a sign of waste in not using your available resources effectively. Or, it could be a sign of waste in not handling relationships properly.

In Chapter Three, we will further discuss the areas of relationships, time and resources as it relates to reorganizing your life. The emphasis, here, is to simply point out that where there is disorder there is waste; and conversely, where there is waste there is disorganization. This will help us to identify when and where we may need to ReOrganize our life.

ReOrganize in Haggai

At the beginning of this chapter, it was mentioned that, the word "re" means again, anew or over again. It was also, stated that the word reorganize means to organize again or anew; to place in order again; return to order; to arrange again; to bring order to again or anew.

As we study the words from Haggai chapter 1 verses 1 through 8, it is very interesting to note that the phrase "consider your ways" from verse five is restated again in verse seven.

The interesting thing, however, is that the word *"consider"* is the same Hebrew word *"sum or sim"* as was discussed in Psalm 50:23, for the word *ordereth*.

As previously stated, the word *ordereth* in the Hebrew language is "sum or sim" {Strong's #7760} [9], and means, to put, to set; establish; to erect; to plant; to make; to constitute; to appoint; to turn; to change; to put something somewhere. *The word ordereth by implication means to organize.*

In substituting our word *"organize"* for the word *"consider"*, we could read Haggai 1:5 as, "Now therefore thus saith the LORD of hosts; <u>Organize</u> your ways".

In addition, we can assume that prior to the time that the word of the LORD came, the ways of the people had some organization or disorganization to it. Thus, when the word of the LORD came it was a word to <u>re</u>organize their ways.

In other words, "Now therefore thus saith the LORD of hosts; Re<u>Organize</u> your ways".

Another interesting thing is that, the word *"ways"* in Haggai verses 5 and 7 is the same Hebrew word *"derek or derekh"*, as was discussed in Psalm 50:23 for the word *"conversation"*.

As indicated, the word *conversation* or *"derek or derekh"* {1870} [10] (in Hebrew) means a going; walk; journey; **way**; path; road; mode; manner; course; **way of life**. The word conversation refers to a course or mode of actions and behaviors in life; in other words, your way of life.

Therefore, Haggai 1:5 could read "Now therefore thus saith the LORD of hosts; Consider your way of life".

Taking the information and definitions for the words above, we could read Haggai 1:5 as "Now therefore thus saith the LORD of hosts; ***ReOrganize your way of life***", ***ReOrganize your ways*** or simply **ReOrganize Your Life**™.

Once you have begun the process of considering your ways, then you are in the proper position to "go up...and build..." as in

Haggai 1 verse 8. You now have positioned yourself to consider the materials that you may need to ReOrganize Your Life™.

When we reorganize we begin to build upon something; we begin to restructure and reorder matters. It is as if we are framing or shaping a house, which may require various materials and effort to accomplish.

Looking back at Haggai 1 verses 2 and 8:

*"Thus speaketh the Lord of hosts, saying, This people say, The time is not come, the time that the Lord's <u>house</u> should be **built**."*

*"<u>Go up</u> to the mountain, and <u>bring wood</u>, and **build** the <u>house</u>; and I will take pleasure in it, and I will be glorified, saith the Lord." [Emphasis added]*

The Word of GOD says to "Go up". You must do it! You must go up. You must go up and go get the necessary materials, information, training, etc. that you may need to build with. In other words, it is your responsibility.

The word "built or build"; according to the Noah Webster's American Dictionary of The English Language [11], means; to frame, construct, and raise, as an edifice or fabric of almost any kind; to unite materials into a regular structure for use or convenience. To frame or shape into a particular form; to raise anything on a support or foundation or to rest on as a foundation.

In Hebrew, the word for build means to make, repair or to set up. To reorganize you will need to make, repair or set up the foundation, which has been neglected.

It's interesting that in the New Testament, the word house generally refers to the people of GOD.

Sometimes in our life we must *"go up to the mountain, and bring wood, and build the house"* We must "go up" to GOD to get what we need to frame, construct, and raise it anew. Sometimes we must unite materials into a regular structure for use or for convenience. And then, we may need to shape matters into a particular form, or to raise it on or to rest it on an existing foundation.

ReOrganize Your Life

When we attempt to do things ourselves, as opposed to GOD doing it, the foundation may shift over time.

Some time ago, I encountered the situation of repairing what appeared to be a minor crack in the wall of a room in our home. The crack was the result of the foundation of the home possibly having settled. In my attempt to do a simple repair, I had to go get the necessary tools and materials to complete the repair.

After doing a "professional" job of filling in the crack I proceeded to sand it down and touch it up to match the other part of the wall. For a while the repair seemed to be good. I was proud of my handiwork. However, over time the crack reappeared in the same exact place, as if I had never repaired it.

This time I got smart, and allowed a real professional to do the repair. I watched to see what I had not done in the process of my repair. Well, among other things, the real professional, proceeded to skillfully tear and remove a portion of the drywall on each side of the crack. After doing this he began to refill the drywall with the appropriate material, applied sandpaper and after retouching it, you could not tell that there was a crack, even after a period of time.

The reason for sharing this brief story of the drywall repair is not to impress you with my handiwork (as if you don't already know this). But I say this, to point out a very important factor of reorganizing. Sometimes you must consult with or bring in a professional, expert or specialist to do the job right!

In other words, sometimes, you must listen to some other person or have another show you how to reorganize.

To reorganize, we must look at ourselves first. We need to look at what we do and how we do it.

ReOrganizing may actually require you to skillfully tear down or remove a portion of the wall to fix the problem.

Dr. Martyn Lloyd-Jones says that, "It seems to me that at least once a year it is a good thing for us to review our position. The danger with all of us is that we simply go on doing our work and become so immersed in it that we are in danger of missing the wood because of the trees. It is a good thing therefore, as far as we can, to stand aside for a moment and look at the whole situation, and particularly as we ourselves stand in relation to it." [12]

Although the statement above was made during an address given by Dr. Lloyd-Jones on June 19, 1963 it is a timeless statement, as is the following statement as it relates to the scripture in Haggai.

Dr. Lloyd-Jones also says "But I think that Haggai chapter one sets before us the present situation, as I see it, that the words of verse 5, repeated in verse 7, are particularly relevant: 'Now therefore thus saith the Lord of hosts; Consider your ways.' The position as described by the prophet is very much the same as it is at the present time, a period of transition, of reconstruction, of new beginnings. Haggai addresses these people in that situation, points out to them their failure, indicates to them what they are doing, and what they are not doing, and in the midst of it there comes this great appeal, 'Consider your ways'." [13]

As Dr. Lloyd-Jones suggests, pointing out your failings indicates what you are, and what you are not doing.

How To Know If You Need To ReOrganize Your Life

How do you know if you need to reorganize an area of your life? This is a very important question to consider.

In general, when there is disorder in your life, it may be a sign of the need to reorganize.

What is disorder? According to the Noah Webster's 1828 Dictionary Software CD; [14]

"DISORDER, n. [dis and order.]

1. Want of order or regular disposition; irregularity; immethodical distribution; confusion; a word of general application; as, the troops were thrown into disorder; the papers are in disorder.
2. Tumult; disturbance of the peace of society; as, the city is sometimes troubled with the disorders of its citizens.
3. Neglect of rule; irregularity...
4. Breach of laws; violation of standing rules, or institutions.

ReOrganize Your Life

5. Irregularity, disturbance or interruption of the functions of the animal economy; disease; distemper; sickness. [See Disease.] disorder however is more frequently used to express a slight disease.

6. Discomposure of the mind; turbulence of passions.

7. Irregularity in the functions of the brain; derangement of the intellect or reason.

DISORDER, v.t.

1. To break order; to derange; to disturb any regular disposition or arrangement of things; to put out of method; to throw into confusion; to confuse; applicable to every thing susceptible of order.

2. To disturb or interrupt the natural functions of the animal economy; to produce sickness or indisposition; as, to disorder the head or stomach.

3. To discompose or disturb the mind; to ruffle.

4. To disturb the regular operations of reason; to derange; as, the mans reason is disordered.

5. To depose from holy orders. [Unusual.]

Disorder is also found in 120 definitions: {*this is only a partial listing of the related definitions mentioned in the Dictionary}

* chaos
* clutter
* confusion
* disarrangement
* disarray
* disease
* disorganized
* disorganizer
* displace
* distraction"

Disorder is basically, the want of order, you may not consciously recognize it, but there will be an inner desire to reorganize.

We can see from the definition, that where there is disorder there is "confusion", "disturbance of the peace", "neglect of rule", "discomposure of the mind", or "disturbance of the regular operations of reason", which may lead to complete chaos or disorganization.

Simply stated, in general, when there is disorder in your life, it may be a sign of the need to reorganize.

To begin to answer the question of "how do you know if you need to reorganize an area of your life"—it is appropriate to seek the answer from a biblical perspective. In doing so, we must go back to the beginnings or the Genesis of all things.

"In the beginning God created the heaven and the earth.

And the earth was without form, and void; and darkness was upon the face of the deep." Genesis 1:1-2a

Essentially, in the beginning, there was disorder upon the face of the earth. In other words, at first, the earth was disorganized. Genesis 1:2a says that the earth was without form, void and dark.

Foundationally it is important to note that, in life, there are three major components of disorder or disorganization.

Three major components of disorder:

1. Without Form
2. Void
3. Darkness

How do you know if you need to ReOrganize Your Life? Primarily, you look for these three major components of disorder.

According to *The Complete Word Study Bible & Reference CD*, the Hebrew definitions and comments for the words above are, in part, as follows:

Without Form: "8414, Tohu; this word comes from an unused Hebrew root. It means desolation, desert ... a desolated city... a worthless thing, confusion, emptiness, vanity ... wasteness (Gen. 1:2 ...) ... This word has no certain parallels in other languages. Therefore, its meaning must be determined entirely from OT contexts. One thing is very clear, tohu has a very negative connotation... "

"1:2 ... the Hebrew construction of verse two is disjunctive, describing the result of the creation described in verse one. The phrase "without form and void" is often misunderstood because of this rendering. These words are found only in a few other places (Is. 34:11; 45:18; Jer. 4:23). They do not describe chaos, but rather emptiness. A better translation would be "unformed and unfilled."

Darkness: "2822, Choshekh; dark, darkness, obscurity, night, dusk; misery, falsehood, ignorance...The term has the figurative meaning of blindness, hiddenness, and judgment ..." [15]

Void: 0922, "Bohuw; from an used root (meaning to be empty)". [16]

If your life is currently without form, void or dark reorganizing your life is something that you should seriously consider, as soon as possible.

Chapter one, verse two of the Amplified Bible reads, in part;

"The earth was without form and an empty waste, and darkness was upon the face of the very great deep." Genesis 1:1-2a

Again, as derived from the 1828 Dictionary, disorder is basically, "the want of order".

Where there is disorder there is "confusion" or "disturbance of the peace", which may lead to complete chaos or disorganization.

Accordingly, as indicated, other characteristics of disorganization are confusion and little peace.

Confusion in one's life may be the direct result of disorder in their life which, in turn, leads to the lack of peace and visa versa.

I believe that confusion cultivates disorder and disorder cultivates confusion.

I say this simply because if you honestly look at, past or current, situations in your own life you will agree. Where there was confusion, disorder was being nourished. Where there was disorder, confusion was being nourished.

We know that the source of confusion and disorder is not from GOD.

"For He [Who is the source of their prophesying] is not a God of confusion {and} disorder but of peace {and} order. As [is the practice] in all the churches of the saints (God's people),"1 Corinthians 14:33 AMP.

In other words, peace is a direct result of order and order is a direct result of peace, in the life of a Godly person.

Where there is disorder there is also idleness or "neglect", which may lead to complete chaos or disorganization.

The bible describes other characteristics of disorder in 2 Thessalonians 3:7 and 11. Disorder does not only exhibit itself in the form of confusion or lack of peace, but people have tendencies of being in disorder when their lives are in a state of idleness or neglectfulness.

People who are idle for extended periods of time or who neglect certain areas of their life for long periods tend to be disorderly.

Another characteristic of disorder is not taking care of your own affairs, but able to find time to be busy with other people's affairs and thus, not taking the time to do the work one needs to do to reorganize their own life.

For you yourselves know how it is necessary to imitate our example, for we were not disorderly {or} shirking of duty when we were with you [we were not idle]. 2 Thessalonians 3:7 AMP

> *"Indeed, we hear that some among you are disorderly [that they are passing their lives in idleness, neglectful of duty], being busy with other people's affairs instead of their own and doing no work." 2 Thessalonians 3:11 AMP*

In short, idleness, neglectfulness, being busy with other people affairs and not your own, and not doing the necessary work to properly ReOrganize Your Life, may be areas for serious attention when considering your ways.

Furthermore, where there is disorder there is also "discomposure of the mind" or "disturbance of the regular operations of reason", which may lead to complete chaos or disorganization in one's life.

Where there is disorder, there is a negative impact upon the mind.

When an individual is disorganized it affects the thought processes of the mind.

No matter what a person may believe, disorder will, to some degree, eventually, impact the composure or disposition of the mind. To put it bluntly, disorder will affect your attitude. Disorder will disturb one's ability to reason in a maximized manner.

Therefore, the Bible admonishes us to be constantly renewed in the spirit of our mind, so that we may always have a fresh mental and spiritual attitude.

> *"And be constantly renewed in the spirit of your mind [having a fresh mental and spiritual attitude]," Ephesians 4:23 AMP*

Earlier we mentioned Haggai chapter one verse five in our discussion of ReOrganizing Your Life™. Here we note how, the Amplified Version reads:

> *Hag 1:5 "Now therefore thus says the Lord of hosts:* **Consider your ways {and} <u>set your mind</u> on what has come to you."** *Haggai 1:5 AMP {emphasis added}.*

Back to Ephesians, the Scripture further tells us to no longer live a disorganized, empty and darkened life, where our mind is negatively affected and our understanding and reasoning is clouded.

What follows is vivid description of person who has allowed their life to continue on an extreme path of a disorganized life.

*"So this I say and solemnly testify in [the name of] the Lord [as in His presence], that you must no longer live as the heathen (the Gentiles) do in their perverseness [in the folly, vanity, and **emptiness of their souls** and **the futility] of their minds**. Their moral **understanding is darkened** {and} their **reasoning is beclouded**. [They are] alienated (estranged, self-banished) from the life of God [with no share in it; this is] because of the ignorance (the want of knowledge and perception, the willful blindness) that is deep-seated in them, due to their hardness of heart [to the insensitiveness of their moral nature]. In their spiritual apathy they have become callous {and} past feeling {and} reckless and have abandoned themselves [a prey] to unbridled sensuality, eager {and} greedy to indulge in every form of impurity [that their depraved desires may suggest and demand]. But you did not so learn Christ!" Ephesians 4:17-20 AMP {emphasis added}*

This is a description of a person whom, in the ultimate sense, has become a disorganized individual. More accurately, this is a description of a person who did not so learn of the LORD JESUS CHRIST and followed Him in living their life.

In summary, to ReOrganize Your Life™, means that you must now consider your ways. You must become intimately familiar with who you are and how you do the things in your life.

You know if you need to reorganize an area of your life if there is disorder in your life

CHAPTER TWO

ROYL Principles ™

Seven ROYL Principles:

1. To ReOrganize Your Life, means that, you must put GOD first.

2. To ReOrganize Your Life, means that, you must now consider your ways.

3. To ReOrganize Your Life, means that, where there is disorder you have some form of waste.

4. To ReOrganize Your Life, means that, there are three major components of disorder; (1) Without Form (2) Void (3) Darkness

5. To ReOrganize Your Life, means that, where there is disorder, there is confusion or a disturbance of the peace.

6. To ReOrganize Your Life, means that, where there is disorder, there is idleness or neglect.

7. To ReOrganize Your Life, means that, where there is disorder, there is a negative impact upon the mind.

CHAPTER THREE

What Areas Do I ReOrganize?

Only let us hold true to what we have already attained {and} walk {and} *order* our lives by that. Philippians 3:16 AMP {Emphasis added}

CHAPTER THREE

What Areas Do I ReOrganize?

In Chapter Two we discussed, in detail, what reorganizing means, its characteristics and "How to Know If You Need to ReOrganize Your Life".

It may be a good idea to go back and read Chapter Two again, so that you can get a clearer picture of the areas you may need to consider for ReOrganizing Your Life

Philippians chapter three, verse sixteen of the Amplified Version of the Scripture tells us to "hold true to what we have already attained {and} walk {and} order our lives by that". In other words, our duty is to whole heartily take the Bible for our guide and order our lives by it; first GOD as our Father, JESUS CHRIST as Savior and LORD and the HOLY SPIRIT as our guide and helper.

I believe that there are four basic areas to hold true to in everyone's life which need our attention, as we seriously consider reorganizing our lives. Again, Philippians says, to hold true to what we have already attained {and} walk {and} *order* our lives by that.

What areas do we reorganize? The four basic areas are: our **doctrine**, our **relationships**, our **resources** and our **time**.

First, To ReOrganize Your Life™, You Must Hold True To *Your Doctrine*.

Your doctrine in life is a primary key to every other area in your life and will dictate how you live and how you ReOrganize Your Life™.

Your doctrine is the foundation for every decision you make in life, directly or indirectly; consciously or unconsciously. Your doctrine determines who you really are.

Your doctrine in life determines what you do with your relationships, your resources, and your time.

Where you receive your doctrine is crucial to the life you live. Being a Christian, it is no secret that I strive to receive my doctrine in life from the Word of GOD.

Surprisingly, most people do not understand how important their doctrine is to their life. The doctrine that one lives by, directly affects the quality of the life you lead.

To say it another way, you lead your life by your doctrine. Your life is led by your doctrine.

Thus, change your doctrine, change your life. ReOrganize your doctrine, ReOrganize Your Life.

If a major change is necessary in your life, look at your doctrine first. Look at what you believe. Some would say look at your "values" in life.

As a side note, I chose the word *doctrine* in this chapter after discernment and very careful consideration. I believe that the word *doctrine* is consistent with rightly dividing the Word of GOD.

Most people, including leaders of prominent christian churches, often avoid the term *doctrine*. This may be because the term may be considered overly harsh, very strong or simply, "extremely" biblical.

Most people, including politically or "theologically" correct christian leaders, inaccurately choose to use more secular terms when referring to doctrine. Those secular terms are the words *values* and *morals*.

"There are forms of "theological correctness" in the church that are really only current opinion that has been inflated with the mantle of theological authority. And this "TC movement" is far from truly correct theologically."[17]

The primary reason for using the term doctrine is that, values and morals in a society may change from generation to generation. Without going into a detailed study, we see this change in the latter part of the 20th century and the beginning of the 21st century in the United States of America, as well as the rest of the world.

While it is good to give consideration to the secularists' understanding of values and morals; and while it is good to have, what secularists may refer to as values and morals, it is no substitution for sound Christian doctrine. Sound Christian doctrine, does not change or expand from generation to generation or from century to century. Your values and morals are a direct result of your doctrine.

> *"Then understood they how that he bade them not **beware** of the leaven of bread, but **of the doctrine of the Pharisees and of the Sadducees**." Matthew 16:12*

If the words "values and morals", are based upon and found within the Word of GOD, then alright; this is practicing virtue for righteousness sake (Philippians 4:8). But this is not necessarily always the case. The Bible does, however, contain instruction on what may be considered values and morals.

As a matter of fact, in rightly dividing the Word of GOD, the terms *values* and *morals*, as used by secularists, is not in the King James Version of the Bible. Where the word value (no "s") is used three times in the New Testament, it is generally referring to worth, i.e. "better than", of honor or to prize (as seen in Matthew 10:3, 27:9 and Luke 12:7).

In defining of the words moral and morality the Noah Webster's 1828 Dictionary, in part, speaks of morals and morality as follows;

> *"MOR'AL, a. ...Relating to the practice, manners or conduct of men as social beings in relation to each other, and with reference to right and wrong. The word moral is applicable to actions that are good or evil, virtuous or vicious, <u>and has reference to the law of God as the standard by which their character is to be determined</u>. The word however may be applied to actions which affect only, or primarily and princi-*

pally, a person's own happiness.

Moral law, <u>the law of God which prescribes the moral or social duties</u>, and prohibits the transgression of them."

"MORAL'ITY, n. <u>The doctrine or system</u> of moral duties, or the duties of men in their social character; ethics. <u>The system of morality to be gathered from the writings of ancient sages, falls very short of that delivered in the gospel</u>.

The quality of an action which renders it good; <u>the conformity of an act to the divine law</u>, or to the principles of rectitude. This conformity implies that the act must be performed by a free agent, and from a motive of obedience to the divine will. <u>This is the strict theological and scriptural sense of morality. But we often apply the word to actions which accord with justice and human laws, without reference to the motives form which they proceed</u>." [18] {Emphasis added}.

The Bible does, indeed, have a lot to say about doctrine, (emphasis added) in the verses which follow:

*"**All scripture is given by inspiration of God, and is profitable for <u>doctrine</u>**, for reproof, for correction, for instruction in righteousness:" 2 Timothy 3:16*

*"**Take heed unto thyself, and unto <u>the</u> <u>doctrine</u>**; continue in them: for in doing this thou shalt both save thyself, and them that hear thee." 1 Timothy 4:16*

*"If any man teach otherwise, and consent not to wholesome words, even the words of our Lord Jesus Christ, and **to <u>the</u> <u>doctrine</u> which is according to godliness**;" 1 Timothy 6:3*

*"Not purloining, but shewing all good fidelity; that they may **adorn <u>the</u> <u>doctrine</u> of God our Saviour in all things**."
Titus 2:10*

*"Till I come, **give attendance** to reading, to exhortation, **to doctrine**." 1 Timothy 4:13*

*"Let the elders that rule well be counted worthy of double honour, especially **they who labour in the word and doctrine**." 1 Timothy 5:17*

*"In all things **shewing thyself a pattern of good works: in doctrine** shewing uncorruptness, gravity, sincerity," Titus 2:7*

*"But **thou hast fully known my doctrine**, manner of life, purpose, faith, longsuffering, charity, patience," 2 Timothy 3:10*

To summarize the above, all scripture is given by inspiration of GOD, and is profitable for doctrine.

We must take heed to the doctrine which is according to godliness, the doctrine of GOD our SAVIOUR.

We must give attendance to this doctrine and show a pattern of good works in this doctrine; for we are fully known by our doctrine.

The implication of all of the above is that, doctrine which is good and sound doctrine is found in the scripture and is profitable to use to ReOrganize Your Life™.

Doctrine which is according to godliness is good and sound doctrine. The Bible goes on to speak of good and sound doctrine:

*"If thou put the brethren in remembrance of these things, thou shalt be a good minister of Jesus Christ, **nourished up in the words of faith and of good doctrine**, whereunto thou hast attained." 1 Timothy 4:6*

*"Holding fast the faithful word as he hath been taught, that he may **be able by sound doctrine both to exhort and to convince** the gainsayers." Titus 1:9*

*"But **speak** thou **the things which become sound <u>doctrine</u>:**"* Titus 2:1

To further the process of ReOrganizing Your Life™, you must be nourished up in the words of faith and of good doctrine so that you may be able by sound doctrine, both to exhort and to convince others. This is done by speaking and applying the things which become sound doctrine according to the Scripture.

"Good" doctrine means biblically righteous or honest. The word "sound" referenced here means healthy. Sound is the Greek word hugiaino (5198, from 5199); which is "to have sound health, i.e. be well (in body); figuratively, to be uncorrupt (true in doctrine): — be in health, (be safe and) sound, (be) whole(-some)". [19]

There are also doctrinal warnings in the Bible:

"For the time will come when they will not endure sound <u>doctrine</u>; but after their own lusts shall they heap to themselves teachers, having itching ears;" 2 Timothy 4:3

*"That we **henceforth be no more children, tossed to and fro, and carried about with every wind of <u>doctrine</u>**, by the sleight of men, and cunning craftiness, whereby they lie in wait to deceive;"* Ephesians 4:14

*"But in vain they do worship me, **teaching for <u>doctrines</u> the commandments of men.**"* Matthew 15:9

*"Howbeit in vain do they worship me, **teaching for <u>doctrines</u> the commandments of men.**"* Mark 7:7

"Wherefore if ye be dead with Christ from the rudiments of the world, why, as though living in the world, are ye subject to ordinances, (Touch not; taste not; handle not;" Colossians 2:20-21

*"Which all are to perish with the using;) after **the commandments and <u>doctrines</u> of men**?"* Colossians 2:22

"But we know that the law is good, if a man use it lawfully; Knowing this, that the law is not made for a righteous man, but for the lawless and disobedient, for the ungodly and for sinners, for unholy and profane, for murderers of fathers and murderers of mothers, for manslayers," 1Timothy 1:8-9
*"For whoremongers, for them that defile themselves with mankind, for menstealers, for liars, for perjured persons, and if there be **any other thing that is contrary to sound doctrine**;" 1Timothy 1:10*

*"Now the Spirit speaketh expressly, that **in the latter times some shall depart from the faith, giving heed to seducing spirits, and doctrines of devils;**" 1Timothy 4:1*

Not only do we need to concern ourselves with doctrine in our life, we need to be assured that our doctrine is good and sound.

The Bible is filled with information on what is good and sound doctrine. Just reading and studying the complete context of the scripture verses quoted above will provide a wealth of foundational information to begin acquiring sound doctrine to ReOrganize Your Life.

Nevertheless, important consideration must be given to avoid unsound doctrine, that is, the unsound doctrine (values or morals) of men and of devils. In First Timothy chapter four we get a glimpse of what is meant, as Paul the Apostle, gives instruction to Timothy.

*"BUT THE [Holy] Spirit distinctly {and} expressly declares that in latter times some will turn away from the faith, giving attention to deluding {and} seducing spirits and **doctrines that demons teach,** Through **the hypocrisy {and} pretensions of liars** whose consciences are seared (cauterized), Who forbid people to marry and [teach them] to abstain from [certain kinds of] foods which God created to be received with thanksgiving by those who believe {and} have [an increasingly clear] knowledge of the truth. For everything God has created is good, and nothing is to be thrown away {or} refused if it is received with thanksgiving. For it is hallowed {and} consecrated by the Word of God and*

*by prayer. If you lay all these **instructions** before the brethren, you will be a worthy steward {and} a good minister of Christ Jesus, ever nourishing your own self on **the truths of the faith** and of the good [Christian] **instruction** which you have closely followed. But **refuse {and} avoid irreverent legends (profane and impure and godless fictions, mere grandmothers' tales) and silly myths, {and} express your disapproval of them. Train yourself toward godliness (piety), [keeping yourself spiritually fit]**. For physical training is of some value (useful for a little), but **godliness (spiritual training) is useful {and} of value in everything {and} in every way**, for it holds promise for the present life and also for the life which is to come. This saying is reliable {and} worthy of complete acceptance by everybody.*

*With a view to this we toil and strive, [yes and] {suffer reproach}, because we have [fixed our] hope on the living God, Who is the Savior (Preserver, Maintainer, Deliverer) of all men, especially of those who believe (trust in, rely on, and adhere to Him). Continue to command these things and to **teach** them. Let no one despise {or} think less of you because of your youth, but be an example (pattern) for the believers in speech, in conduct, in love, in faith, and in purity.*

*Till I come, devote yourself to [public and private] reading, to exhortation (preaching and personal appeals), and to **teaching** {and} instilling **doctrine**. Do not neglect the gift which is in you, [that special inward endowment] which was directly imparted to you [by the Holy Spirit] by prophetic utterance when the elders laid their hands upon you [at your ordination]. Practice {and} cultivate {and} meditate upon these duties; throw yourself wholly into them [as your ministry], so that your progress may be evident to everybody.*

*Look well to yourself [to your own personality] and to [your] **teaching**; persevere in these things [hold to them], for by so doing you will save both yourself and those who hear you. 1Timothy 4:1-16 AMP {Emphasis added}*

Let's not, too quickly, pass by what the bottom line is for the verses above from verse sixteen; look well to your own life and to your doctrine; persevere in sound doctrine which is godliness, for by so doing you will save both yourself and those who hear you.

When the Bible speaks of doctrine it is always in the singular tense of the word. This is most likely, because, "God's word is ONE DOCTRINE. It is not a collection of diverse and separate 'doctrines'. The whole doctrine of God is made up of many, many teachings and this is how the student should view the Bible. Its variety of contents are inextricably linked but, more than that, the separate parts make one organic, dynamic whole." "Doctrine is the stuff of life and of dynamic faith." "Get to grips with doctrine and apply it to your life and your soul will soar heavenward!" [20]

The word doctrines, in the plural tense of the word, is used only in the New Testament and speaks of the doctrines of men and devils (Matthew 15:9, Mark 7:7, Colossians 2:22, 1 Timothy 4:1).

At this point you may be asking, well then, what actually is doctrine.

Doctrine, in a general sense, is simply the teaching, instruction, principle or learning of an individual or group. It is the foundation, support or action of a belief system. Such as in the biblical sense, "the doctrine which is according to godliness" (1Timothy 6:3), with its foundation, support and action in the truth of the Word of GOD.

As used in the New Testament of Scripture the words for doctrine are the Greek words didaskalia and didache.

> "**Doctrine**, *Greek* **didaskalia** *(did-as-kal-ee'-ah), 1319 from 1320; instruction (the function or the information):—doctrine, learning, teaching.*
> *1320. didaskalos (did-as'-kal-os) from 1321; an instructor (genitive case or specially):—doctor, master, teacher.*
> *1321. didasko (did-as'-ko) a prolonged (causative) form of a primary verb dao (to learn); to teach (in the same broad application):—teach.*"

> "**Doctrine**, *Greek* **didache** *(did-akh-ay') 1322, from 1321; instruction (the act or the matter):—doctrine, hath been taught."* [21]

Why is teaching, instruction or principle important? "Why is doctrine important? If our Christian faith is built upon sound and unchanging doctrinal pillars as set forth by God in His Word, then we will not be "carried about with every wind of doctrine" (Eph. 4:14). As instructed in 2 Timothy 3:10, if a Christian is well grounded in sound doctrine, then he or she will not be deceived by false teachers and every new cult that comes along." [22]

In a broad sense, Christian doctrine is essentially the teaching and learning concerning the attainment of salvation through JESUS CHRIST (Luke 1:2, Acts 8:4, 11:1, 14:25, 16:32 AMP) and the transforming (Romans 12:1-2) or ReOrganizing of one's life.

It is my opinion that there are two basic categories of doctrine; *beliefs* and *conduct*. Since this publication is focused primarily on Christian principles, I will briefly provide examples of what is meant.

The two basic categories of Christian doctrine are, what I refer to as, the: 1). Foundation of Christian faith (beliefs) and 2). Foundation of Christian works (conduct). Simply, an individual's doctrine is comprised of what one believes and what one does. The two actually go hand in hand.

However, what one believes may not always be consistent or correspond with what one does.

> *"What doth it profit, my brethren, though a man say he hath faith, and have not works? can faith save him?*
> *If a brother or sister be naked, and destitute of daily food,*
> *And one of you say unto them, Depart in peace, be ye warmed and filled; notwithstanding ye give them not those things which are needful to the body; what doth it profit?*
> *Even so **faith, if it hath not works**, is dead, being alone.*
> ***Yea, a man may say, Thou hast faith, and I have works: shew me thy faith without thy works, and I will shew thee my faith by my works.***

Thou believest that there is one God; thou doest well: the devils also believe, and tremble.
*But wilt thou know, O vain man, that **faith without works** is dead?*
Was not Abraham our father justified by works, when he had offered Isaac his son upon the altar?
Seest thou how faith wrought with his works, and by works was faith made perfect?
And the scripture was fulfilled which saith, Abraham believed God, and it was imputed unto him for righteousness: and he was called the Friend of God.
Ye see then how that by works a man is justified, and not by faith only.
Likewise also was not Rahab the harlot justified by works, when she had received the messengers, and had sent them out another way?
*For as the body without the spirit is dead, so **faith without works is dead** also." James 2:14-26 {Emphasis added}*

In short, faith (beliefs) without corresponding works (conduct) is lifeless.

When beliefs (faith) and conduct (works) are not consistent or does not correspond, one may be referred to as a hypocrite.

Doctrinal examples of the foundation of Christian faith (beliefs):

Since Christian doctrine is a detailed and expansive topic, I will simply mention and direct the reader to a publication called The Essentials of the Christian Faith by Craig Hawkins. Professor Hawkins states that "There are *at least* five Essential doctrines of the Gospel". This is what I refer to as doctrinal examples of the Foundation of Christian Faith (beliefs):

"To be an Essential doctrine or teaching, it must be explicitly (clearly) taught in a verse or passage of Scripture—and stated as such—and/or be entailed or inferred directly from a verse, verses, passage, or passages of Scripture alone.

They are not simply the opinion or view of a given Christian denomination, pastor, teacher, theologian, etc."

"Essential Doctrines:

1. Salvation by Grace Alone Through Faith Alone
2. Christ's Vicarious Atonement (The Penal Substitutionary View)
3. The Bodily Resurrection of Christ Jesus from the Dead
4. The Unique Deity (and Humanity) of Jesus Christ
5. The Trinity" [23]

Now doctrinal examples of the Foundation of Christian Works (conduct).

First, let me clearly state that, I am not referring to works as being that which we can be saved through. To the contrary, I firmly believe that by grace are we saved through faith; and that not of ourselves, salvation is the gift of God and not of works (Ephesians 2:8-9).

I am referring to the behavior we should all strive towards once we have the gift of salvation through JESUS CHRIST. In other words, acts of righteousness.

These acts of righteousness or the behavior which is produced from the fruit of the character of the individual is significant when speaking of Christian works or conduct.

*"But the **fruit** of the [Holy] Spirit [the **work** which His presence within accomplishes] is love, joy (gladness), peace, patience (an even temper, forbearance), kindness, goodness (benevolence), faithfulness,*
Gentleness (meekness, humility), self-control (self-restraint, continence). Against such things there is no law [that can bring a charge].

And those who belong to Christ Jesus (the Messiah) have

crucified the flesh (the godless human nature) with its passions and appetites {and} desires.

*If we live by the [Holy] Spirit, let us also walk by the Spirit. [If by the Holy Spirit we have our life in God, let us go forward walking in line, our **conduct** controlled by the Spirit.]*

Let us not become vainglorious {and} self-conceited, competitive {and} challenging {and} provoking {and} irritating to one another, envying {and} being jealous of one another." Galatians 5:22-26 AMP {emphasis added}

Christian works or conduct is produced as a tree produces its fruit. But, the quality of the fruit is dependent upon the condition of its root.

The Christian walk is to be fruitful and rich, producing (distributing and communicating) good works and increasing in the knowledge of GOD.

"That ye might walk worthy of the Lord unto all pleasing, being fruitful in every good work, and increasing in the knowledge of God;" Colossians 1:10

"Charge them that are rich in this world, that they be not highminded, nor trust in uncertain riches, but in the living God, who giveth us richly all things to enjoy;

That they do good, that they be rich in good works, ready to distribute, willing to communicate;

Laying up in store for themselves a good foundation against the time to come, that they may lay hold on eternal life." 1 Timothy 6: 17-19

Reference is made to works that are manifested as a result of the fruit of the HOLY SPIRIT working in us. Not that which is merely the morals or values of a politically correct society that may change from generation to generation or century to century.

Let me close this section on doctrine with instruction and an admonition from the Word of GOD:

"Whosoever transgresseth, and abideth not in the doctrine of Christ, hath not God. He that abideth in the doctrine of Christ, he hath both the Father and the Son.

If there come any unto you, and bring not this doctrine, receive him not into your house, neither bid him God speed:

For he that biddeth him God speed is partaker of his evil deeds." 2 John 1: 9-11

"Whom shall he teach knowledge? and whom shall he make to understand doctrine? them that are weaned from the milk, and drawn from the breasts.

For precept must be upon precept, precept upon precept; line upon line, line upon line; here a little, and there a little:" Isaiah 28:9-10

Doctrine should not be taken lightly. It should be ReOrganized into our life, in an orderly fashion to set a solid foundation; precept upon precept, line upon line; here a little, and there a little, as we grow throughout our lifetime.

Second, To ReOrganize Your Life™, You Must Hold True To *Your Relationships.*

Your relationships are a vital element when consideration is given to ReOrganize Your Life™.

GOD established relationships as a vital element of our lives. The Bible says that, in the Beginning, GOD made man in His image and likeness. GOD created mankind, male and female, in His own image (Genesis 1:26-27). I believe that GOD did this to allow for a relationship with mankind and to allow for relationships among mankind.

I believe, also, that GOD established a priority of structure as well as obligations, duties and responsibilities within those relationships.

The first relationship priority which must be considered and established when you ReOrganize Your Life is the right relationship with GOD, our LORD JESUS CHRIST.

The Bible admonishes us to seek first the kingdom of GOD, and his righteousness and all the other things of life shall be added to you (Matthew 6:33).

The only way to seek first the kingdom of GOD and His righteousness is a right relationship through JESUS CHRIST, as SAVIOUR and LORD of our life.

*"Let not your heart be troubled: ye believe in God, believe also in me." "Jesus saith unto him, **I am the way**, the truth, and the life: **no man cometh unto the Father, but by me."** John 14:1, 6 (emphasis added)*

The right relationship with GOD is vital and cannot be accomplished through our humanistic or secular acts and deeds nor through the Law or by the laws of man. It is the walk of faith.

*"For Christ is the end of the Law [the limit at which it ceases to be, for the Law leads up to Him Who is the fulfillment of its types, and in Him the purpose which it was designed to accomplish is fulfilled. That is, the purpose of the Law is fulfilled in Him] as the means of righteousness (**right relationship to God**) for everyone who trusts in {and} adheres to {and} relies on Him." Romans 10:4 AMP (emphasis added)*

*"For we walk by faith [we regulate our lives and conduct ourselves by our conviction or belief respecting **man's relationship to God** and divine things, with trust and holy fervor; thus we walk] not by sight {or} appearance." 2 Corinthians 5:7 AMP (emphasis added)*

You must walk by faith in GOD; you must first ReOrganize Your Life and conduct yourself by your conviction or belief in establishing and respecting a right relationship with GOD.

In the previous section on "your doctrine", we saw the importance of faith and here also, faith plays a significant role in living our life.

*"But the just shall live by faith [My righteous servant shall live by his conviction respecting **man's relationship to God** and divine things, and holy fervor born of faith and conjoined with it]; and if he draws back {and} shrinks in fear, My soul has no delight {or} pleasure in him." Hebrews 10:38 AMP (emphasis added)*

And the good news is that:

*Therefore, since we are now justified (acquitted, made righteous, and brought into **right relationship with God**) by Christ's blood, how much more [certain is it that] we shall be saved by Him from the indignation {and} wrath of God. Romans 5:9 AMP (emphasis added)*

So what is a relationship anyway? According to Noah Webster's 1828 Dictionary, it is "the state of being related by kindred, affinity or other alliance". [24]

We are able to be in right relationship with GOD by and through CHRIST. In other words, we are allowed to be a relative of GOD or related by kindred, affinity and alliance because of the blood, death and resurrection of CHRIST.

To increase our understanding, there are four words of interest as defined in the Noah Webster's 1828 Dictionary when discussing matters of relationship. First of all, the word relationship, as used here, is taken in context as a noun from the word relative.

"REL'ATIVE, n. 1. A person connected by <u>blood or affinity</u>; <u>strictly, one allied by blood</u>; a relation; a kinsman or kinswoman.
2. <u>That which has relation to something else</u>."

"CONSANGUINITY, n. [L., blood.] The <u>relation of persons by blood</u>; the relation or connection of persons descended from the same stock or common ancestor, in distinction from affinity or relation by marriage. It is lineal or collateral.."

"AFFIN'ITY, n. [L. affinitas, from affinis, adjacent, related by marriage; ...]
1. The <u>relation contracted by marriage</u>, between a husband and his wife's kindred, and between a wife and her husband's kindred; <u>in contradistinction from consanguinity</u> or relation by blood. Solomon made affinity with Pharaoh. 1Kings 3.
2. <u>Agreement</u>; relation; conformity; resemblance; connection; ..."

"ALLI'ANCE, n. [Gr.; L.] 1. The relation or union between families, <u>contracted</u> by marriage.
2. The union between nations, <u>contracted</u> by compact, treaty or league.
3. The <u>treaty, league, or compact</u>, which is the instrument of confederacy; sometimes perhaps the act of confederating.
4. <u>Any union or connection of interests</u> between persons, families, states or corporations; as, an alliance between church and state.
5. The <u>persons or parties allied</u>; as, men or states may secure any alliances in their power." [25] (Emphasis added)

In short, there are three basic methods in which one comes into relationship with another:

1. relationship of consanguinity; the relation of persons by blood or ancestry.

2. relationship of affinity; the relation of persons by marriage covenant.

3. relationship of alliance; the relation of persons by agreement, compact or interests, etc.

Of course, there may be a combination of the three basic methods. Based upon the Scriptures, as stated earlier, because of the blood, death and resurrection of JESUS CHRIST, Christians are allowed a relationship of consanguinity, a relationship of affinity and a relationship of alliance with GOD (Ephesians 2:13, Matthew 26:28, Mark 14:24, Hebrews 9:20, Matthew 22:9, Ephesians 5:22-32, Hebrews 13:11, Revelation 19:7, 9).

The second relationship priority which must be considered and established when you ReOrganize Your Life™ is the marriage relationship.

The first human relationship established by GOD was one of marriage between Adam and Eve (husband and wife).

"And God blessed them, and God said unto them, Be fruitful, and multiply, and replenish the earth, and subdue it: and have dominion over the fish of the sea, and over the fowl of the air, and over every living thing that moveth upon the earth." (Genesis 1:26-28)

God blessed <u>them</u> and said to <u>them</u>. The word <u>them</u> implies that there is to be a relationship.

To be fruitful, multiply, replenish, subdue and have dominion requires a relationship between "them".

In Genesis Chapter 2 verse 18, "…the LORD God said, It is not good that the man should be alone; I will make him an help meet for him."

The words <u>help meet</u>, again, implies that there is to be a relationship. A help meet in Hebrew, means; an aid or helper. To be a true aid or helper to another requires the establishment of a relationship.

"And the LORD God caused a deep sleep to fall upon Adam and he slept: and he took one of his ribs, and closed up the flesh instead thereof;

And the rib, which the LORD God had taken from man, made he a woman, and brought her unto the man.

And Adam said, This is now bone of my bones, and flesh of my flesh: she shall be called Woman, because she was taken out of Man.

Therefore shall a man leave his father and his mother, and shall cleave unto his wife: and they shall be one flesh." Genesis 2:21-24

"Wives, submit yourselves unto your own husbands, as unto the Lord. For the husband is the head of the wife, even as Christ is the head of the church: and he is the saviour of the body. Therefore as the church is subject unto Christ, so let the wives be to their own husbands in every thing. Husbands, love your wives, even as Christ also loved the church, and gave himself for it; That he might sanctify and cleanse it with the washing of water by the word, That he might present it to himself a glorious church, not having spot, or wrinkle, or any such thing; but that it should be holy and without blemish. So ought men to love their wives as their own bodies. He that loveth his wife loveth himself. For no man ever yet hated his own flesh; but nourisheth and cherisheth it, even as the Lord the church: For we are members of his body, of his flesh, and of his bones. For this cause shall a man leave his father and mother, and shall be joined unto his wife, and they two shall be one flesh. This is a great mystery: but I speak concerning Christ and the church. Nevertheless let every one of you in particular so love his wife even as himself; and the wife see that she reverence her husband." Ephesians 5:22-33

If you are married, after your doctrine, the next area to look at to ReOrganize Your Life™ is your marriage relationship. This means that there must be a commitment to honor, work and grow together in your marriage.

It means that you must "leave", "cleave" and ReOrganize Your Life to be "one flesh".

The third relationship priority which must be considered and established when you ReOrganize Your Life is the children relationship.

The second human relationship established by GOD was the relationship with your children.

> *"And Adam knew Eve his wife; and she conceived, and bare Cain, and said, I have gotten a man from the LORD.*
>
> *And she again bare his brother Abel. And Abel was a keeper of sheep, but Cain was a tiller of the ground." Genesis 4:1-2*
>
> *"And Adam knew his wife again; and she bare a son, and called his name Seth: For God, said she, hath appointed me another seed instead of Abel, whom Cain slew.*
>
> *And to Seth, to him also there was born a son; and he called his name Enos: then began men to call upon the name of the LORD." Genesis 4:25-26*

I believe that GOD allowed each of us to be born into a certain family for His purpose in ministering to and within that particular family unit.

I further believe that GOD gave each of us certain talents and abilities which in turn allows for the most effective prayer and passion for those in that family unit. Thus, I believe that the next priority we have in relationships is that of children.

> *"And Manoah arose, and went after his wife, and came to the man, and said unto him, Art thou the man that spakest unto the woman? And he said, I am.*
> *And Manoah said, Now let thy words come to pass.* **How shall we order the child**, *and how shall we do unto him?" Judges 13:11-12 {Emphasis added}*
>
> *"One that ruleth well his own house, having his children in subjection with all gravity;*
> *(For if a man know not how to rule his own house, how shall he take care of the church of God?)" 1 Timothy 3:4-5*

"But if any provide not for his own, and specially for those of his own house, he hath denied the faith, and is worse than an infidel." 1 Timothy 5:8

"Train up a child in the way he should go: and when he is old, he will not depart from it." Proverb 22:6

"Children, obey your parents in the Lord: for this is right. Honour thy father and mother; (which is the first commandment with promise;) That it may be well with thee, and thou mayest live long on the earth. And, ye fathers, provoke not your children to wrath: but bring them up in the nurture and admonition of the Lord." Ephesians 6:1-4

Although the instruction on ruling the household, in 1 Timothy 3:4-5, is directed at the man who desires the office of a bishop (overseer), the principle is one that is applicable to all men in general.

We see in 1 Timothy 5:8, that this principle is taken a step further. A person who does not provide for their own household or family denies their faith in the Gospel and is worse than an unbeliever.

Training up your children in the proper path or course in life is a duty of parents. Teaching your children and showing (by conducting your own life properly) is a great responsibility given by GOD. Parents are given the task of influencing and molding the future character of their children.

This is accomplished by not provoking them to wrath, but by bringing them up in the nurture and admonition of the LORD (Ephesians 6:4).

That is, do not dictate unreasonable and severe commands to the child that reinforce the manifestation of anger. But show love by the proper disciplinary correction or chastening and instruction, as well as calling attention to the improper behavior with mild rebuke or warning.

The end result is that things in life will tend to go well and a long life to accomplish the will of GOD, for children who obey their parents (in the LORD) and who honor their parents.

Within each family there is the direct potential for GOD to establish His will through the prayer, ministry and training of those in that respective family.

For where two or three are gathered together in my name, there am I in the midst of them. Matthew 18:20

As I have experienced with my son, Ray Jr., it is quite rewarding when your son does not depart from the way and even asks for counsel from his dad. The honor received from children is truly a blessing.

The fourth relationship priority which must be considered and established when you ReOrganize Your Life™ is the extended family relationship.

The third human relationship established by GOD was the relationship with your extended family. By extended family, I mean father, mother, brother, sister, grandparents, and other relatives as led by GOD.

Why is it, that GOD mentions the various genealogies throughout the Scriptures? The "family tree" is a factor in what GOD does through that particular family.

"Honour thy father and mother; (which is the first commandment with promise;) That it may be well with thee, and thou mayest live long on the earth." Ephesians 6:2-3

It is important to have the proper Godly relationship with those members of our extended family, so that GOD can use us in accomplishing His will in the lives of our extended family members.

Joseph was a great example of how GOD is able to use family members to do His will within that family and for His people as a whole.

"And Joseph said unto his brethren, Come near to me, I pray you. And they came near. And he said, I am Joseph your brother, whom ye sold into Egypt. Now therefore be not grieved, nor angry with yourselves, that ye sold me hither: for God did send me before you to preserve life." Genesis 45:4-5

"And God sent me before you to preserve you a posterity in the earth, and to save your lives by a great deliverance. So now it was not you that sent me hither, but God: and he hath made me a father to Pharaoh, and lord of all his house, and a ruler throughout all the land of Egypt. Haste ye, and go up to my father, and say unto him, Thus saith thy son Joseph, God hath made me lord of all Egypt: come down unto me, tarry not: And thou shalt dwell in the land of Goshen, and thou shalt be near unto me, thou, and thy children, and thy children's children, and thy flocks, and thy herds, and all that thou hast: And there will I nourish thee; for yet there are five years of famine; lest thou, and thy household, and all that thou hast, come to poverty." Genesis 45:7-11

"And Pharaoh said unto Joseph, Say unto thy brethren, This do ye; lade your beasts, and go, get you unto the land of Canaan; And take your father and your households, and come unto me: and I will give you the good of the land of Egypt, and ye shall eat the fat of the land." Genesis 45:17-18

Just consider for a moment; if each person within the extended family was open to and allowed for other family members to teach and minister to them on what the Scripture says.

The fifth relationship priority which must be considered and established when you ReOrganize Your Life is the relationship within the Body of Christ.

The fourth human relationship established by GOD was the relationship within the body of Christ. That is, the Church of GOD, which is under the authority of JESUS CHRIST as head.

"And I say also unto thee, That thou art Peter, and upon this rock I will build my church; and the gates of hell shall not prevail against it." Matthew 16:18

"Now ye are the body of Christ, and members in particular." 1Corinthians:12:27

"Submitting yourselves one to another in the fear of God.

Wives, submit yourselves unto your own husbands, as unto the Lord. For the husband is the head of the wife, even as Christ is the head of the church: and he is the saviour of the body. Therefore as the church is subject unto Christ, so let the wives be to their own husbands in every thing. Husbands, love your wives, even as Christ also loved the church, and gave himself for it; That he might sanctify and cleanse it with the washing of water by the word, That he might present it to himself a glorious church, not having spot, or wrinkle, or any such thing; but that it should be holy and without blemish. So ought men to love their wives as their own bodies. He that loveth his wife loveth himself. For no man ever yet hated his own flesh; but nourisheth and cherisheth it, even as the Lord the church: For we are members of his body, of his flesh, and of his bones. For this cause shall a man leave his father and mother, and shall be joined unto his wife, and they two shall be one flesh. This is a great mystery: but I speak concerning Christ and the church. Nevertheless let every one of you in particular so love his wife even as himself; and the wife see that she reverence her husband." Ephesians 5:21-33

GOD has set the members in the Church, the body of CHRIST, as it pleased Him (1Corinthians 12:18). Relationships are established and reorganized in order to accomplish His will in the kingdom of GOD.

GOD establishes certain people with certain gifts, abilities and talents (spiritually and naturally) to minister to our needs.

As a pastor, when I would have occasion to teach before various groups, I would often say that each one of us have some special or unique gift that GOD has given us, to help bring about His will, in that particular place and at that particular time.

The sixth relationship priority which must be considered and established when you ReOrganize Your Life is the relationship with friends and acquaintances.

The fifth human relationship established by GOD was the relationship with friends and acquaintances. Your neighbors, fellow workers, people we meet day to day in life are an instrumental part of our life. How we interact with one another is a determining factor in how we mature in this life.

> *"And he spake this parable unto them, saying, What man of you, having an hundred sheep, if he lose one of them, doth not leave the ninety and nine in the wilderness, and go after that which is lost, until he find it? And when he hath found it, he layeth it on his shoulders, rejoicing. And when he cometh home, he calleth together his friends and neighbours, saying unto them, Rejoice with me; for I have found my sheep which was lost. I say unto you, that likewise joy shall be in heaven over one sinner that repenteth, more than over ninety and nine just persons, which need no repentance." Luke 15:3-7*

Throughout our life time GOD allows certain paths of people to cross.

As you walk along the path of life, certain individuals you interact with have potentially something within them to offer you for growth. This may be by way of information, experience or some other assistance which can be used to help ReOrganize Your Life.

This is why the Bible admonishes us to love our neighbor as ourselves; and that love does not work ill to his neighbor. In addition, we read; owe no man any thing, but to love one another (Romans 13:8-10).

What if everyone truly desired to, and did not, intentionally, do harm to any other person? Consider for a moment what influence this would have on our relationships in every area of our lives.

We should always remember that, in some way or another we may one day need our neighbor.

To sum it all up;

> *"For the whole Law [concerning human relationships] is complied with in the one precept, You shall love your neighbor as [you do] yourself." Galatians 5:14 AMP*

Third, To ReOrganize Your Life™, You Must Hold True To *Your Resources*.

Your resources provide you with the ability and the means to accomplish things in life.

Resources are an avenue on which we travel toward the goals we set in life

Unfortunately, too often, some goals are set indirectly by others or through circumstances, since we do not proactively assert ourselves in setting our own goals.

In essence, you have certain resources available to you to maintain and to help you ReOrganize Your Life. GOD has given us many resources in life in order to do His will on earth.

According to the 1828 Dictionary, a resource is; "1. **Any source of aid or support**; an expedient to which a person may resort for assistance, safety or supply; means yet untried; resort. An enterprising man finds resources in his own **mind**...
2. Resources, in the plural, pecuniary means; funds; **money** or any **property** that can be converted into **supplies**; means of raising money or supplies. Our national resources for carrying on war are abundant. Commerce and manufactures furnish ample resources." [26] (Emphasis added)

As we see, resources come in all forms; for instance, prayer is a great resource, as well as, your mind, food and other nourishment, your health, clothing, property, money, your talents, work and so many other things.

> *"And Joseph nourished his father, and his brethren, and all his father's household, with bread, according to their families." Genesis 47:12*

Resources are the supplies or goods utilized to carry out matters of life. Resources are used to support, maintain, and provide for our lives and others. As such, our resources must be reorganized, sometimes, on a regular basis.

We know that certain resources are necessary to sustain our life in this world. However, to keep things in perspective and with the proper priority, we are to "take no thought" nor say what shall we eat, or drink or how shall we be clothed?

When it comes to ReOrganizing Your Life, our priority cannot always be on talking about the necessities in life. GOD knows that we have need of those things.

Instead, our focus must be on utilizing and reorganizing the other resources provided by our Heavenly Father, the first being on seeking GOD.

"Therefore take no thought, saying, What shall we eat? or, What shall we drink? or, Wherewithal shall we be clothed? (For after all these things do the Gentiles seek:) for your heavenly Father knoweth that ye have need of all these things. But seek ye first the kingdom of God, and his righteousness; and all these things shall be added unto you.
Take therefore no thought for the morrow: for the morrow shall take thought for the things of itself. Sufficient unto the day is the evil thereof." Matthew 6:31-34

Resources are natural (or material) and spiritual in nature, which includes our talents and gifts given to us by GOD.

Resources are comprised of the goods, talents and abilities given or made available to us by GOD. But GOD expects us to be good stewards in the trading of those resources.

GOD has called each of us to be stewards or managers of the affairs of our life. Thus, He expects us to properly manage those resources available to us (Luke 12:42, 16:2).

"And the Lord said, Who then is that faithful and wise steward, whom his lord shall make ruler over his household, to give them their portion of meat in due season?" Luke 12:42

Everyone is called to be steward over the affairs of their life and GOD has given you the ability to do so. Besides, no one can manage the affairs of your life accept you. Others can help or teach you how to reorganize matters, but you are ultimately responsible for how you manage the resources of your life.

A steward is, simply, one who manages on behalf of someone else. Since GOD owns it all (Psalm 24:1, 1Corinthians 10:26, Deuteronomy 10:14), we are but stewards or servants of His property.

> *"For the kingdom of heaven is as a man travelling into a far country, who called his own servants, and delivered unto them his goods. And unto one he gave five talents, to another two, and to another one; to every man according to his several ability; and straightway took his journey. Then he that had received the five talents went and traded with the same, and made them other five talents. And likewise he that had received two, he also gained other two. But he that had received one went and digged in the earth, and hid his lord's money."* Matthew 25:14-18

Resources are, also, supplies which may be available to help others. And, in deed, are given to help others.

> *"But by an equality, that now at this time your abundance may be a supply for their want, that their abundance also may be a supply for your want: that there may be equality: As it is written, He that had gathered much had nothing over; and he that had gathered little had no lack."* 2Corinthians 8:14-15

Available resources play a very significant role when you ReOrganize Your Life™.

Fourth, To ReOrganize Your Life™, You Must Hold True To Your Time.

Holding true to your time is crucial when it comes time to ReOrganize Your Life.

Chapter 7 of the Book of Job begins with an appropriate question about time;

> *"Is there not an appointed time to man upon earth? are not his days also like the days of an hireling?"* Job 7:1

In Chapter 3 of the Book of Ecclesiastes, we find an appropriate answer to this question;

"To every thing there is a season, and a time to every purpose under the heaven:" Ecclesiastes 3:1

The point is that we all have an appointed amount of time upon this earth and with that appointed time we must seize upon the various seasons in our life to accomplish the purposes established at that particular stage in life.

Life is built upon seasons and times. Life is comprised of seasons and time and it involves a process which produces growth on the road to maturity.

"And he shall be like a tree planted by the rivers of water, that bringeth forth his fruit in his season; his leaf also shall not wither; and whatsoever he doeth shall prosper." Psalms 1:3

In the process of time we bring forth fruit, which is the evidence of the type of life we live.

"And in process of time it came to pass, that Cain brought of the fruit of the ground an offering unto the LORD. And Abel, he also brought of the firstlings of his flock and of the fat thereof. And the LORD had respect unto Abel and to his offering:" Genesis 4:3-4

Seasons are simply, units of time. Every one is familiar with winter, spring, summer and fall and how these units of time affect our lives— how we must even adjust some of the routines and functions of life depending upon the season.

"And God said, Let there be lights in the firmament of the heaven to divide the day from the night; and let them be for signs, and for seasons, and for days, and years:" Genesis 1:14

It is said that, time is one of the most important resources that we have. In fact, time is one of the most valuable elements of life. Time is, also, one of the only nonnegotiable elements in our lives. We can only reorganize what we do with it and when it is gone it cannot be replenished.

> *"While the earth remaineth, seedtime and harvest, and cold and heat, and summer and winter, and day and night shall not cease." Genesis 8:22*

What you put your time into now will pay positive or negative dividends in your future. To put it in a biblical way, "you will reap what you sow" with your time.

Real choices in life are about time choices—that is, what you do with your time in the present will affect what your future will be. What you do today will impact your life five, ten, twenty, thirty, forty or fifty years from now.

It is said that, Ben Franklin once said, *"You may delay, but time will not"*.

Author Os Guinness, says that, "Time is our final currency in life and all the money in the world can't give us extra seconds, minutes, or days." [27]

When we speak about what we do with our time, there are many things that we can do with our time while we have it.

There are several fundamentals of the process of time or time organization, but I will only briefly mention five.

Five Fundamentals of Time Organization:
There is a Time of laying foundations
There is a Time of setting goals
There is a Time of preparation
There is a Time of action
There is a Time of reorganizing

Think of these fundamentals of time as an ongoing cycle, where it continues depending upon the season you are in or approaching.

The Time of laying foundations:
This is a time for building character, establishing disciplines, principles, doctrine and unity.

The Time of setting goals:
This is a time to determine what it is that you want to accomplish. It is a time to focus on your desires.

The Time of preparation:
This is a time to listen, read and follow wise instructions and advice given by mentors.

The Time of action:
This is a time to perform and follow through on the things learned. It is a time of hard work.

The Time of reorganizing:
This is a time to evaluate your accomplishments, and make the necessary adjustments for the coming season in the cycle of time.

Time is an opportunity for accomplishment. But, when all is said and done it is about wisdom. Wisdom in the choices you make with your time and how you live your life.

There is a proverb in the Bible which says;

"Wisdom is the principal thing; therefore get wisdom: and with all your getting get understanding." Proverb 4:7

"Listen to advice and accept instruction, that you may gain wisdom for the future." Proverb 19:20 ESV

Use the seasons and time in your life as an investment towards your future.

Successes in life comes from the effective use of the seasons and time given to us all, by GOD. Therefore, you must know what season you are in and take the time for *laying the foundation,* take the time for *setting goals*, take the time for *preparation*, take the time for *action* and take the time for *reorganizing* your life.

Most people at some point in their life probably have said, "If I could go back in time, I would have…or … I wouldn't have". Everything comes back to time.

"How then do we redeem time, and how are we redeemed from time? On one hand, we redeem the time by living out our lives according to our gifts and callings, thus serving God's purposes in our generation. Those who live out their lives in this way do justice to the best of their time; and they live before all time because they live before God.

On the other hand, we redeem time by trusting the end of our time to the Lord and redeemer of time. Ultimately, we redeem the time and are redeemed from time only through the one who is the redeemer of everything—He who is, the God who is the Lord of time and history and yet is "the same yesterday, today, and forever."[28]

It is through GOD and GOD alone that time is redeemed. Ephesians Chapter five says:

> *"See then that ye walk circumspectly, not as fools, but as wise, Redeeming the time, because the days are evil. Wherefore be ye not unwise, but understanding what the will of the Lord is." Ephesians 5:15-17*

Redeeming the time means, to rescue or recover our time from wasteful things. Use time for wise purposes and not foolishly. In these evil days there are many distractions and temptations that easily lead us from the proper and wise use of our time. Understanding the will of the LORD is strategic to how you use your time.

To ReOrganize Your Life you must maintain an appropriate balance with how time is used. Once time, as we know it, is lost it cannot be recovered. You cannot go back and recycle time.

An important fact to always remember is that, you cannot manage time, you can only manage or reorganize how you choose to use the time you have. You can reorganize what you do with your time.

How you use time will impact your life forever. What we do with the time we have will determine our eternity.

"There is one point in which all of us are the same that may be illustrated in the following way. Let's say a bank credited to your account every day $86,400 without fail. Yet the bank carried over no balance from day to day, and so allowed you to keep no cash in your account. What was not used of the $86,400 was lost by day's end, yet for the next day you had a new credit in your account. This is exactly what happens to each of us as God credits to our account each day 86,400 seconds of time. We either use time properly or we lose it, for the day cannot be relived again. Each day is a new day with new opportunities, but once we move through the day our record stands." "No person alive can say he has "no time", for time is the one thing we all have equally." [29]

Time is an opportunity for accomplishment.

"Then Jesus said unto them, My time is not yet come: but your time is alway ready." John 7:6

The common bond in each of the four basic areas; your doctrine, your relationships, your resources and your time is GOD, our LORD JESUS CHRIST and the HOLY SPIRIT. Without this bond in your life, your life itself is incomplete and disorganized.

CHAPTER THREE

ROYL Principles ™

Seven ROYL Principles:

1. To ReOrganize Your Life, whole heartily take the Bible for your guide and order your life by it.

2. To ReOrganize Your Life, hold true to your doctrine.

3. To ReOrganize Your Life, hold true to your relationships.

4. To ReOrganize Your Life, hold true to your resources.

5. To ReOrganize Your Life, hold true to your time.

6. To ReOrganize Your Life, take the time for; laying the foundation, setting goals, preparation, action and reorganizing.

7. To ReOrganize Your Life, change your doctrine, change your life. ReOrganize your doctrine, ReOrganize Your Life.

CHAPTER FOUR

The Essentials For ReOrganizing

Where there is no vision, the people perish: but he that keepeth the law, happy is he. Proverbs 29:18

CHAPTER FOUR

The Essentials For ReOrganizing

Where there is no vision in the life of people, most seem to allow nearly any thing to happen. When you have no plan for certain areas of your life you will tend to become idle and disorganization is on its way.

You Need Vision

To ReOrganize Your Life™ you need vision. You need to be able to see what path you are on in different areas of your life. You need to know where you are headed and where you want to be.

Day after day of "visionlessness" will create months or years of disorder in that part of your life. Where you have no vision, gradually you will allow yourself to become disorganized.

The consequence of having no vision (or as I say, "visionlessness") is an area that will need reorganizing at some point sooner or later in life.

Although *"visionlessness"* is not a word in dictionaries, I choose to use the word to highlight the possible negative affect of *having no vision* and to stress the importance of the need of vision in certain areas of life.

My definition of the term visionlessness is; "having no vision for your life, thus leading to disorganization or chaos in an area of one's life. Visionlessness causes the need to ReOrganize Your Life in that particular area."

For example, I am convinced that obesity is a factor in most people lives because there is "visionlessness"; they have no healthy and dedicated vision in that part of their life, thus disorder rules in that part of life. The answer is to ReOrganize Your Life™ in that area.

Individuals who have a dedicated vision for losing weight have reorganized their life and are usually successful in reaching their goal. Their vision is alive and well.

Having said that, I am equally convinced that some people are content with being obese, but one thing is certain; they have a dedicated vision operating in their life which reorganizes their life toward accomplishing their goal.

In actuality, you may have order in one or more areas of your life, while in another or other areas there is disorder. This is simply, often, due to not having a vision for those areas.

"Where there is no vision, the people perish: but he that keepeth the law, happy is he." Proverbs 29:18

"Where there is no vision, the people cast off restraint; But he that keepeth the law, happy is he." Proverbs 29:18 ASV

The second portion of Proverbs 29:18 is critical in our understanding about vision. That is, he that keeps the law is happy. So, let's discuss the meaning of the words "vision", "perish", "keepeth", "law" and "happy".

The word **vision**, is the Hebrew word; "chazown (*khaw-zone'*) (2377) which means a sight (mentally), i.e. a dream, revelation, or oracle:—vision and is from the word chazah (*khaw-zaw'*) (2372) a primitive root word meaning; to gaze at; mentally, to perceive, contemplate (with pleasure); specifically, to have a vision of:—behold, look, prophesy, provide, see." [30]

The word **perish**, is the Hebrew word; "para` (*paw-rah'*) (6544), a primitive root word meaning; to loosen; by implication, to expose, dismiss; figuratively, absolve, begin:—avenge, avoid, bare, go back, let, (make) naked, set at nought, perish, refuse, uncover." [31]

The word **keepeth**, is the Hebrew word; "shamar (*shaw-mar'*) (8104) a primitive root word meaning; properly, to hedge about (as with thorns), i.e. guard; generally, to protect, attend to, etc.:—beward, be circumspect, take heed (to self), keep(-er, self), mark, look narrowly, observe, preserve, regard, reserve, save (self), sure, (that lay) wait (for), watch(-man)." [32]

The word **law**, is the Hebrew word; "(towrah (*to-raw'*) (8451) or torah {to-raw'}; meaning a precept or statute, especially the Decalogue or Pentateuch:—law; from the word yarah (*yaw-raw'*) (3384) or (2 Chr. 26:15) yara; {yaw-raw'}; a primitive root; properly, to flow as water (i.e. to rain); transitively, to lay or throw (especially an arrow, i.e. to shoot); figuratively, to point out (as if by aiming the finger), to teach:—(+) archer, cast, direct, inform, instruct, lay, shew, shoot, teach(-er,-ing), through." [33]

The word **happy**, is the Hebrew word; "'esher (*eh'-sher*) (835), meaning; happiness; only in masculine plural construction as interjection, how happy!:—blessed, happy; and is from the word 'ashar (*aw-shar'*) or rasher {aw-share'} (833), a primitive root; to be straight (used in the widest sense, especially to be level, right, happy); figuratively, to go forward, be honest, proper:—(call, be) bless(-ed, happy), go, guide, lead, relieve." [34]

Using the definitions above we could illustrate what is stated in Proverbs 29:1 in this manner; where there is no mental sight, revelation, perception or provision, people are loose, exposed, uncovered and go backward in life. The person who properly guards or takes heed to themselves and marks or attends to the precepts or instruction of the Word of GOD, is blessed, right, goes forward and is properly guided in life.

Where there is vision people receive and use instruction, information or knowledge to flourish in that part of their life. Where there is no vision people live loosely, without restraint, thereby exposing and uncovering them in that area of life which becomes wilted. That area of life is on a downward slope of dying as a result of visionlessness.

As stated previously, the second portion of Proverbs 29:18 is crucial to our understanding of vision. The bottom line is, if you want to be happy in life start by getting a vision for certain areas of your life. In other words, you may need to ReOrganize Your Life™.

Our key to happiness is having a vision for our life. Vision is an essential way for reorganizing your life. Have a vision for what you want to accomplish. You need a vision.

Getting a vision for a particular area of your life may be as simple as remembering those thoughts (mental pictures), dreams and desires that you have. Of course I am speaking of pure and honest things. We all have thoughts, dreams and desires of what would make us happy; how we would be blessed and how we could be a blessing.

Taking the time to pray and meditate before GOD will bring illumination to the areas needing to be reorganized.

You might be asking, so then what must I do next? Well, keep reading!

If, however, you still have not identified areas of your life that you may need to reorganize, I suggest that you review Chapters Two and Three.

If you have identified area(s) to reorganize, then take the time right now to write down a word or short sentence describing the area(s) that you need to develop a vision for. It could be a relationship, health, finances, home, a room, work, time or anything.

You Need Understanding and Wisdom

Once you have a vision, you need understanding and wisdom.

"Wisdom is the principal thing; therefore get wisdom: and with all thy getting get understanding." Proverbs 4:7

Next, you need understanding and wisdom about the vision you have. You must acquire as much understanding and wisdom as possible in a reasonable time frame, in order to effectively and skillfully ReOrganize Your Life™.

Wisdom is the principle thing, which is or should be the goal in handling any matter in life. As you strive to have wisdom, regarding your vision, in the process get understanding.

To get understanding and wisdom you first need to acquire knowledge in that specific area identified.

Knowledge is easily available in numerous informational forms (i.e. the Bible, people, books, the Internet, seminars, other media, etc.). The important thing is getting understanding and wisdom on how to use the information and knowledge obtained.

The acquisition of knowledge is dormant energy, getting understanding is the ignition and the use of wisdom is the power for ReOrganizing Your Life.

Knowledge is the acquisition of information, facts and data. However, knowledge in and of itself is useless and benefits no one when not used properly. You must ignite the knowledge with understanding to get wisdom, the power to produce your desired results.

"Get wisdom, get understanding: forget it not; neither decline from the words of my mouth." "Forsake her not, and she shall preserve thee: love her, and she shall keep thee." "Wisdom is the principal thing; therefore get wisdom: and with all thy getting get understanding." "Exalt her, and she shall promote thee: she shall bring thee to honour, when thou dost embrace her." Proverbs 4:6-8

Often when the Old Testament mentions understanding (particularly in the Proverbs) it also mentions two other words; wisdom and knowledge. [Proverbs 2:1-6, 10-11; 3:4-14, 19-22; 9:10; 10:13-14; 24:3-7 {Colossians 1:9}].

Understanding is the connection between knowledge and wisdom.

"Through wisdom is an house builded; and by understanding it is established: And by knowledge shall the chambers be filled with all precious and pleasant riches. A wise man is strong; yea, a man of knowledge increaseth strength." Proverbs 24:3-5

Through wisdom you build your life and by understanding you establish it; by knowledge the inner most parts of your life are filled.

A wise person is strong, but a person of knowledge increases the strength of the wisdom they have.

The word understanding in Proverbs 24:3 is from the Hebrew root word "biyn (bene) (995), which means; to separate mentally (or distinguish)..." [35]

An interesting note is that, as we refer back to our definition for the word vision, it also makes mention of mental sight. Thus we can clearly see the direct connection between vision and understanding.

Understanding essentially means to mentally distinguish, arrange, consider or view; to put it simply; to mentally organize. It is the mental ability to reorganize knowledge.

This is what understanding is; it is the process of mentally organizing a vision for your doctrine, your relationships, your resources and your time.

Now what are the dictionary definitions of knowledge, understanding and wisdom? Let's once again see how the Webster's 1828 Dictionary defines these terms:

"**Knowledge**, n. nol'lej.
1. A clear and certain perception of that which exists, or of truth and fact; the perception of the connection and agreement, or disagreement and repugnancy of our ideas...Human knowledge is very limited, and is mostly gained by observation and experience. 2. Learning; illumination of mind... 3. Skill; ... 4. Acquaintance with any fact or person... 5. Cognizance; notice... 6. Information; power of knowing." [36]

"**Understand'ing**, n.
1. The faculty of the human mind by which it apprehends the real state of things presented to it, or by which it receives or comprehends the ideas which others express and intend to communicate. The understanding is called also the intellectual faculty. It is the faculty by means of which we obtain a great part of our knowledge... that faculty whereby we are enabled to apprehend the objects of knowledge, generals or particulars, absent or present, and to judge of their truth or falsehood, good or evil." [37]

"**Wisdom**, n. s as z. [G. See Wise.]
1. The right use or exercise of knowledge; the choice of laudable ends, and of the best means to accomplish them. This is wisdom in act, effect, or practice. If wisdom is to be considered as a faculty of the mind, it is the faculty of discerning or judging what is most just, proper and useful, and if it is to be considered as an acquirement, it is the knowledge and use of what is best, most just, most proper, most conducive to prosperity or happiness... wisdom is the exercise of sound judgment either in avoiding evils or attempting good... Wisdom gained by experience, is of inestimable value." [38]

"**Wise**, a. s as z. [G., to know., L.]
1. Properly, having knowledge; hence, having the power of discerning and judging correctly, or of discriminating between what is true and what is false; between what is fit and proper, and what is improper; ... 2. Discrete and judicious in the use or applications of knowledge; choosing laudable ends, and the best means to accomplish them." [39]

Now, allow me to give you my short meaning of these words:

Knowledge is the clear perception, learning, or information about that which exists.

Understanding is the means by which we mentally apprehend, receive, or comprehend knowledge.

Wisdom is the right use, exercise or application of our understanding.

Some people have the mistaken idea that an individual whom may be gifted as an organizer just walks into a group of people, a room or some matter and without much effort, the next thing you know everything is orderly.

Reorganizing is a process which begins with mentally assimilating or arranging sound knowledge by getting a sound understanding of the knowledge and using sound wisdom to successfully apply the results.

My formula I recommend to ReOrganize Your Life™ is: sound knowledge + sound understanding + sound wisdom = a sound vision (or as abbreviated: sK+ sU+sW=sV).

An important fact is that, you cannot have understanding without first acquiring knowledge.

However, your understanding may be flawed since it is dependent upon the knowledge you acquired. Your understanding is only as good as the knowledge you have. Even so, with understanding it is implied that there exists some level of knowledge.

In addition, your wisdom may be flawed since it is dependent upon your understanding. Your wisdom is only as good as the understanding you have. You may have simply drawn the wrong conclusion from your understanding.

In other words, your wisdom may be void of understanding. Having said this lets look at Proverbs Chapter 24:

> *"I went by the field of the slothful, and by the vineyard of the man void of understanding; And, lo, it was all grown over with thorns, and nettles had covered the face thereof, and the stone wall thereof was broken down. Then I saw, and considered it well: I looked upon it, and received instruction. Yet a little sleep, a little slumber, a little folding of the hands to sleep: So shall thy poverty come as one that travelleth; and thy want as an armed man." Proverbs 24:30-34*

These verses are normally used to bring attention to the unfruitfulness of the slothful or lazy person. And it does point this out, but reading verse 30 in it entirety, we see that it makes reference also of the man who is void of understanding. *"I went by the field of the slothful, <u>and</u> by the vineyard of the man void of understanding;"*

We fail to understand that, mentioned here are two categories of people—the slothful and the void of understanding—whose life produces the same type of outcome, unfruitfulness or disorder.

Disorder is eventually the fruit of a slothful (lazy) person and the person void of understanding.

The lazy person and the person void of understanding is one who lacks the initiative to mentally apprehend, receive, or comprehend knowledge or to use wisdom for getting a sound vision in their life.

The result of a lazy person or a person void of understanding is no productive vision. We see in verse 31 the disorder; thorns, nettles and the walls of life broken down.

Is your life filled with "thorns", "nettles" and "brokenness"? Is there a lot of clutter or chaos in an area of your life? If so, this may be a sign that you need to ReOrganize Your Life™!

Well then, consider and receive the instruction as is stated in verses 32 and 33, that is; idleness in an area of your life may lead to disorder.

You must wake up, or that area of your life will become gradually impoverished or destitute (disorganized). Disorder will come upon you step by step every hour coming nearer and nearer into your life as an armed person, difficult to stop.

By now you may be saying, well how do I get more understanding to help ReOrganize my life? The short answer is the Word of GOD, by meditating on the testimonies of GOD's Word.

"I have more understanding than all my teachers: for thy testimonies are my meditation" Psalm 119:99

If you want to cultivate understanding to ReOrganize Your Life™ then meditate on what GOD says, follow the commandments of the LORD.

Meditation means to mentally image, to mentally ponder and consider, and consistently speak it. Again we see a direct connection with our previous definitions for vision and understanding.

According to *Joshua 1:8* you shall have good success, if you meditate and observe to do what is written.

"This book of the law shall not depart out of thy mouth; but thou shalt meditate therein day and night, that thou mayest observe to do according to all that is written therein: for then thou shalt make thy way prosperous, and then thou shalt have good success." Joshua 1:8

Your vision must become part of you by meditating on it and then doing it.

Psalm 49:3 says that you will speak wisdom and understanding will be of your heart, as a result of your meditation.

"My mouth shall speak of wisdom; and the meditation of my heart shall be of understanding." Psalm 49:3

A primary part of reorganizing your life, is a matter of meditation, of pondering, of considering all of the information, facts, etc.; for the purpose of putting them into a functional arrangement or order, thus getting a vision for an area of your life.

It may be from GOD's Word in combination with natural information and facts; this is how you begin to ReOrganize Your Life.

Most people are disorganized because they either do not meditate on anything or they simply fantasize, daydream or worry; in effect meditating on something unproductive.

If you think about it; those things that you really like to meditate on, you probably are more organized at.

The point is that, you must begin by meditating on ReOrganizing your doctrine, or your relationships, or your resources, or your time or some combination of these general areas of your life.

I believe that it is essential for us to ReOrganize our life. ReOrganize, so that we can accomplish what GOD wants us to accomplish.

GOD will give you the wisdom you need, if you ask in faith, not wavering or being double minded about what it is that you want to do.

"If any of you lack wisdom, let him ask of God, that giveth to all men liberally, and upbraideth not; and it shall be given him." "But let him ask in faith, nothing wavering. For he that wavereth is like a wave of the sea driven with the wind and tossed." "For let not that man think that he shall receive any thing of the Lord." "A double minded man is unstable in all his ways." James 1:5-8

GOD will give you all the knowledge, the understanding and wisdom you need.

"As for these four children, God gave them knowledge and skill in all learning and wisdom: and Daniel had understanding in all visions and dreams." "And the king communed with them; and among them all was found none like Daniel, Hananiah, Mishael, and Azariah: therefore stood they before the king." "And in all matters of wisdom and understanding, that the king enquired of them, he found them ten times better than all the magicians and astrologers that were in all his realm." Daniel 1:17, 19, 20

There is one major caution, that of relying upon our own abilities alone. It is summed up in Proverbs Chapter 3:

"Trust in the Lord with all thine heart; and lean not unto thine own understanding." "In all thy ways acknowledge him, and he shall direct thy paths." Proverb 3:5-6:

Don't lean to your own ability to ReOrganize Your Life™, but trust in the LORD and He will direct your path.

As a believer, we have the HOLY SPIRIT (the Spirit of wisdom, understanding and knowledge, according to Isaiah 11:2), as our helper.

It's part of His responsibility to help you ReOrganize Your Life™. It is simply a matter of yielding and trusting in GOD.

But where shall we find wisdom and understanding?

"But where shall wisdom be found? and where is the place of understanding?"

"Man knoweth not the price thereof; neither is it found in the land of the living."

"It cannot be gotten for gold, neither shall silver be weighed for the price thereof."

"No mention shall be made of coral, or of pearls: for the price of wisdom is above rubies."

"Whence then cometh wisdom? and where is the place of understanding?"

"God understandeth the way thereof, and he knoweth the place thereof."

"And unto man he said, Behold, the fear of the Lord, that is wisdom; and to depart from evil is understanding." Job 28:12, 13, 15, 18, 20, 23, 28

All true understanding and wisdom comes from GOD.

You Need To Write It

Now you need to write your vision down. Get a vision, write it plainly, read it, and then run to go get it.

You must be able to see in writing where it is that you want to go and what it is that you want to do or be. It is very important for you write it down.

"I will stand upon my watch, and set me upon the tower, and will watch to see what he will say unto me, and what I shall answer when I am reproved." "And the LORD answered me, and said, Write the vision, and make it plain upon tables, that he may run that readeth it." "For the vision is yet for an appointed time, but at the end it shall speak, and not lie: though it tarry, wait for it; because it will surely come, it will not tarry." "Behold, his soul which is lifted up is not upright in him: but the just shall live by his faith." Habakkuk 2:1-4

Let's dissect verse 2, above:

The word **write** is the Hebrew word kathab (*kaw-thab'*) (3789) a primitive root word which means to grave, by implication, to write (describe, inscribe, prescribe, subscribe): —describe, record, prescribe, subscribe, write(-ing, -ten). [40]

The word **plain** is the Hebrew word ba'ar (*baw-ar'*) (874) a primitive root which means to dig; by analogy, to engrave; figuratively, to explain: —declare, (make) plain(-ly). [41]

The word **tables** is the Hebrew word luwach (*loo'-akh*) (3871)or luach {loo'-akh} from a primitive root; probably meaning to glisten; a tablet (as polished), of stone, wood or metal: —board, plate, table. [42]

The word **run** is the Hebrew word ruwts (*roots*) (7323) a primitive root which means to run (for whatever reason, especially to rush): —break down, divide speedily, footman, guard, bring hastily, (make) run (away, through), post. [43]

The word **readeth** is the Hebrew word qara' (*kaw-raw'*) (7121) which is a primitive root word which means... to call out to (i.e. properly, address by name,...) mention, (give) name, preach, (make) proclaim (-ation), pronounce, publish, read, renowned, say. [44]

We see that our vision must be described by engraving and explaining it upon good durable material to make it look polished, so that you can move in the direction to achieve it as you call out, proclaim and publish what your vision is.

The primary reason for writing your vision down, is that you must first mentally see and know, in your mind, the expected ending from the beginning. This is what you are actually doing when you begin to write your vision down.

"Better is the end of a thing than the beginning thereof: and the patient in spirit is better than the proud in spirit."
Ecclesiastes 7:8

It then becomes important to keep in mind that accomplishing your vision will take time, so patience is required. You must realize that certain barriers and habits must be broken, allowing you to stay on the path of your vision.

"For the vision is yet for an appointed time, but at the end it shall speak, and not lie: though it tarry, wait for it; because

it will surely come, it will not tarry." "Behold, his soul which is lifted up is not upright in him: but the just shall live by his faith." Habakkuk 2:3-4

Although there may be some delay, your vision will surely come to pass; if you adhere to it by staying on course and if you have patience enough to wait for it. There is an appointed time period which is necessary for accomplishing your vision. But you must have faith in reaching for the mark.

To ReOrganize Your Life you must begin to set forth in order your markings for your vision. Declare what you believe in writing. Arrange your vision so that it can become a certainty in your life.

"Forasmuch as many have taken in hand to set forth in order a declaration of those things which are most surely believed among us," "Even as they delivered them unto us, which from the beginning were eyewitnesses, and ministers of the word;" "It seemed good to me also, having had perfect understanding of all things from the very first, to write unto thee in order, most excellent Theophilus," "That thou mightest know the certainty of those things, wherein thou hast been instructed." Luke 1:1-4 {emphasis added}

To "set forth in order" means to compose a narrative. The above verse then, goes on to mention to "write in order" or to describe in an organized manner, from your understanding.

The way to do this is to establish your vision marks (commonly referred to as goals, etc.). But to start with, you must forget the past disorder in your life. Put the past disorder behind you, reach for the new marks of order in your, soon to be, Reorganized life. Let your vision come to life.

*"Brethren, I count not myself to have apprehended: but this one thing I do, forgetting those things which are behind, and reaching forth unto those things which are before," "I press toward the **mark** for the prize of the high calling of God in Christ Jesus." Luke 3:13-14 {emphasis added}*

As you press toward the mark, GOD will, in the course of time, move on your behalf and through you as you set in order your declared vision, and as you walk in the high calling of GOD; the commandments of the LORD.

"And it came to pass, that while he executed the priest's office before God in the order of his course," Luke 1:8

So far, we have discovered that, to ReOrganize Your Life™ involves a process of having a vision, getting the necessary understanding and wisdom and then setting forth that vision by writing it down.

You Need Systems

Next, you need systems to help you ReOrganize Your Life. Creating a system or systems will assist you in staying on track with your vision. A system is also needed to increase the likelihood that you will accomplish your vision.

A system helps you simplify the needed actions of your vision.

This is one of the critical areas that most individuals leave out or do not spend the appropriate amount of time or effort on, when attempting to ReOrganize their life.

Know where you want to be and then ReOrganize, setting up systems to get you there.

Making a system will remind you of the important elements that must be completed on the path to ReOrganize Your Life. Making a system will ensure that the important elements are actually completed at the appointed time.

Now that you have your vision, you have understanding and wisdom and you have committed your vision to writing, it's time to become a system-maker. A system-maker is simply one who forms a system. Create your own system for reaching and pressing toward the vision marks you have established.

A system is:
"1. An assemblage of things adjusted into a regular whole; or a whole plan or scheme consisting of many parts connected in such a manner

ReOrganize Your Life

as to create a chain of mutual dependencies; or a regular union of principles or parts forming one entire thing. 2. Regular method or order." [45]

A system is your vision assembled into smaller parts or a scheme, a method or checklist which sets forth the order for accomplishing your vision to ReOrganize Your Life™.

Your system will be the parts connecting your way to assembling and completing your vision. It can be as simple as writing a checklist of the various steps that are necessary.

One of my most favorite hobbies is flying the various jets on the Microsoft Flight Simulator computer program.

The Airline Industry, particularly aircraft pilots and Air Traffic Control is one of the most organized man made systems we have in operation each hour of our lives.

As stated in Chapter 1, pilots use checklists for flying their respective aircraft. The checklists contain the steps needed for pre-start, startup, before taxi, taxi, before take-off, after take-off, climb, cruise, descent, approach, taxi to ramp, shutdown and securing the aircraft.

Take-off Checklist Illustration* [46]:
Smoothly increase thrust to 40% N1 let spool up
Takeoff Thrust — FULL
Brakes — RELEASE
V1 = 120 KIAS (decision)
Vr = 130 KIAS (rotate)
Pitch — 10-15 degrees, nose up
V2 = 140 KIAS (safety)
At Positive Climb Rate — Touch Brakes
Landing Gear — RETRACT
At 210 KIAS — RETRACT flaps up

(*Not intended to be an exact Learjet checklist)

ReOrganize Your Life

As you can see a checklist is something short and to the point, describing what is to happen at a given point in time and the order of occurrence.

An important reason for establishing systems is that, having a system creates consistency in that area of life. The lack of consistency tends to, sometimes, bring disorder.

In order to ReOrganize Your Life you need to become consistent at completing the new vision for that area of your life. Having a system or systems will help establish the consistency needed.

As a former basketball player at Central Michigan University, I became aware of the importance of creating a system for consistency purposes, when shooting free throws. As a matter of fact, all great free throw shooters have created their own system which is followed each time they go to the line.

When fouled, prior to going to the free throw line the great free throw shooter has already mentally viewed their "free throw checklist" completed countless times before.

If the shooter spins the ball, bends, bounces it three times and then squats before shooting, he will do the exact same thing in the same order, with the same rhythm each and every time. This becomes even more important in the fourth quarter as the shooter relies upon "the system" in spite of the pressure and fatigue.

The great free throw shooter is so consistent at following their system of shooting free throws that it has become a habit. This is what you should strive to achieve when you set out to ReOrganize Your Life™; a habit of a ReOrganized area of life.

A habit is a system in your life which operates instinctively, under the radar of your conscious mind.

It is said that it takes approximately 21 days to form a habit. Conversely, it takes at least 21 days to break or change a habit.

Making your system is the major consideration here. But once you have a ReOrganized system in operation you must understand that, "in a system, small deviations can result in large changes. This concept is now known as the Butterfly Effect." [47]

The "Butterfly Effect" was a term which, reportedly, describes a theory inadvertently discovered by meteorologist Edward Lorenz in the 1960's.

In short, while conducting an experiment Mr. Lorenz inadvertently entered the wrong data into a computer program for the purpose of forecasting the weather. After realizing that the outcome was quite different than expected, he discovered that instead of entering numbers up to the millionth position (for example, 0.748293), he entered numbers to the thousandth position (for example, 0.748).

This inadvertent, but seemingly slight, deviation produced a substantial change in the weather system forecasted. Thus, the term "Butterfly Effect" has created phrases such as; a butterfly flapping its wings in Hawaii could lead to a storm in Michigan.

In other words, a slight change in a system can potentially make a big difference in the overall outcome of that system.

The significant point of raising the "Butterfly Effect" here, as it relates to ReOrganizing Your Life™ is that, even when making a slight change or deviation in your behavior in one area, can result in a substantial change in the quality of your life in general. The result could have a positive or negative effect as you ReOrganize Your Life™ depending upon the changes made.

Begin by making a system for the area of life you want to change. Make adjustments to the system, as necessary, using understanding and wisdom to avoid any negative effects.

Again, know where you want to be and then ReOrganize Your Life™ by setting up systems to get you there.

CHAPTER FOUR

ROYL Principles ™

Seven ROYL Principles:

1. To ReOrganize Your Life, you need sound vision; (sK+sU+sW=Sv).

2. To ReOrganize Your Life, you need understanding and wisdom.

3. To ReOrganize Your Life, you need to meditate on your vision and then do it.

4. To ReOrganize Your Life, you need to write it.

5. To ReOrganize Your Life, you need to establish vision marks.

6. To ReOrganize Your Life, you need systems.

7. To ReOrganize Your Life, you need checklists.

CHAPTER FIVE

Five Easy Steps To Stay ReOrganized

The *steps of a good man are ordered* by the LORD: and he delighteth in his way. Psalms 37:23 {Emphasis added}

CHAPTER FIVE

Five Easy Steps To Stay ReOrganized

A s you go through life you need to have an effective and efficient way, to stay ReOrganized.

After you have activated your system for your vision to ReOrganize Your Life™, there are five easy steps to stay ReOrganized.

The first step is to prioritize, the second step is to examine, the third step is to focus, the fourth step is to pursue and the fifth step is to manage. You must occasionally prioritize and examine your life, while you consistently focus, pursue and manage your life, that is, if you want to stay ReOrganized.

The primary reason to prioritize, examine, focus, pursue and manage is to strive to maintain balance in your life. Having a balanced life reduces stress and confusion, while adding a sense of contentment and joy to living.

First and foremost, a prerequisite to everything is that you should allow the LORD to order your steps.

"The steps of a good man are ordered by the LORD: and he delighteth in his way."
"Though he fall, he shall not be utterly cast down: for the

LORD upholdeth him with his hand." Psalms 37:23-34

"Thou hast enlarged my steps under me; so that my feet did not slip." 2Samuel 22:37

"The law of his God is in his heart; none of his steps shall slide." Psalms 37:31

"A man's heart deviseth his way: but the LORD directeth his steps." Proverbs16:9

So, the first priority or prerequisite to all priorities is to try to always remain open to listen to the LORD, on all matters in your life.

Allowing the LORD to direct your steps will enlarge your opportunity for success. You may follow your heart in devising your way, but let the LORD direct your steps. Disappointments might come, you might come up against some tragedy or unfortunate situation but it will not keep you from accomplishing what you have set out to do.

Steps are simply a way to accomplish something by having a set of instructions or directions to follow.

Throughout our lives there are times when we must follow certain steps or instructions to complete something; on our jobs, cooking with a recipe, driving our vehicles, using our ATM cards, as well as in many other areas of life.

Sometimes we may purchase an item which calls for certain steps to follow for properly using or assembling the item. We usually find that if we follow the steps given for using or assembling the item, it is much easier to accomplish the task.

Prioritize

The first step to stay ReOrganized is to prioritize. Seek first to prioritize the important matters in your life; that is, those things which should take precedence. Of course, as stated above, seeking GOD is the prerequisite to everything (Matthew 6:33).

ReOrganize Your Life

In using the term prioritize, I mean to give precedence in place or rank to the essential matters on any given day, week, month, or year.

Have you, ever or recently, sat down to list what your priorities are in life?

While there are certain general priorities which should be common to all, it is difficult to list or tell you what your respective specific priorities should be. Your specific priorities are individually determined based upon the essential matters at that particular point in your life.

Once you have determined what those essential matters are, you can then rank them in some meaningful order.

As you prioritize matters, you should, also, allow for the unexpected. For instance, when you are to be at a certain destination at a certain time, build into your schedule the possibility of delays. In other words, give yourself some flexibility.

Prioritizing means to put most of your time and effort on the first things. Concentrate on the "one thing" at that specific time which needs to be accomplished.

JESUS CHRIST was a person who set priorities in HIS life. HIS priority or the "one thing", while on earth, was the salvation of mankind. Thus, HIS steps on the path of salvation included "to go to Jerusalem".

> *"From that time forth began Jesus to shew unto his disciples, how that he must go unto Jerusalem, and suffer many things of the elders and chief priests and scribes, and be killed, and be raised again the third day." Matthew 16:2*

> *"And it came to pass, when the time was come that he should be received up, he stedfastly set his face to go to Jerusalem," Luke 9:51*

> *"And he went through the cities and villages, teaching, and journeying toward Jerusalem." Luke 13:22*

JESUS also informed others of the "one thing" at that given point in their life which was a priority for them. Remember that, the first priority or prerequisite to all priorities is to try to always remain open to listen to the LORD.

*"Then Jesus beholding him loved him, and said unto him, **One thing** thou lackest: go thy way, sell whatsoever thou hast, and give to the poor, and thou shalt have treasure in heaven: and come, take up the cross, and follow me." Mark 10:21{emphasis added}*

*"Now when Jesus heard these things, he said unto him, Yet lackest thou **one thing**: sell all that thou hast, and distribute unto the poor, and thou shalt have treasure in heaven: and come, follow me." Luke 18:2 {emphasis added}*

*"But **one thing** is needful: and Mary hath chosen that good part, which shall not be taken away from her." Luke 10:42 {emphasis added}*

Too many people try to do too many things at once, calling it multi-tasking, instead of realizing that "one thing" should be their focus. There are times for multi-tasking, but you must discern when to do it and when not to multi-task.

Sometimes, the "one thing" to do is to forget those things from your past, so that you can reach and apprehend those things which are in front of you (Philippians 3:13).

Success in ReOrganizing Your Life is a direct result of you properly setting your priorities.

To prioritize you may need to take the time to examine the whole matter. Take the time to look at and analyze the big picture of your life and what it is that you are doing.

Examine

The second step to stay ReOrganized is to examine. Take the necessary time to periodically examine your life. That is, inspect, scrutinize or just think about matters in your life.

When you seriously examine your life you should do it with a view of discovering truth or the real state of your life. Truthfully take an inventory of the current situation of your life.

Perform a "SWOT" analysis of your life. "SWOT" is referred to in the business world as an analysis of the Strengths, Weaknesses, Opportunities and Threats related to an operation or venture. This may require that you take the time to privately view the walls of opportunities in your life. That is, what are the positive and the negative situations in your life?

> *"And I arose in the night, I and some few men with me;* **neither told I any man what my God had put in my heart to do** *at Jerusalem: neither was there any beast with me, save the beast that I rode upon." "And I went out by night by the gate of the valley, even before the dragon well, and to the dung port, and* **viewed the walls** *of Jerusalem, which were broken down, and the gates thereof were consumed with fire." "Then I went on to the gate of the fountain, and to the king's pool: but there was no place for the beast that was under me to pass." "Then went I up in the night by the brook, and* **viewed the wall**, *and turned back, and entered by the gate of the valley, and so returned." "And* **the rulers knew not whither I went, or what I did**; *neither had I as yet told it to the Jews, nor to the priests, nor to the nobles, nor to the rulers, nor to the rest that did the work." "Then said I unto them, Ye* **see the distress** *that we are in, how Jerusalem lieth waste, and the gates thereof are burned with fire:* **come, and let us build up the wall** *of Jerusalem, that we be no more a reproach." Nehemiah 2:12-17 {emphasis added}*

View the walls of opportunities in your life and then work toward building upon those walls. The framework already exists, however, sometimes all you need to do is to begin to privately examine and build.

As you examine your life there are a few main considerations in doing so; set a time to examine, be open to the LORD examining you, examine yourself, and realize that others will examine you.

Set a time to examine.

"And the children of the captivity did so. And Ezra the priest, with certain chief of the fathers, after the house of their fathers, and all of them by their names, were separated, and sat down in the first day of the tenth month to examine the matter." Ezra 10:16

Again, take the time to examine the whole matter. Take the time to look at and analyze the big picture of your life and what it is that you are doing.

Be open to the LORD examining you.

"Examine me, O LORD, and prove me; try my reins and my heart." Psalms 26:2

Let the LORD examine your heart. Sometimes we have the wrong motives for doing things in life. Therefore, it is necessary that we keep our hearts open as we pursue our vision. Let the LORD prove or confirm your steps.

Examine yourself.

"But let a man examine himself, and so let him eat of that bread, and drink of that cup." 1 Corinthians 11:28

"Examine yourselves, whether ye be in the faith; prove your own selves. Know ye not your own selves, how that Jesus Christ is in you, except ye be reprobates?" 2 Corinthians 13:5

It is your responsibility to occasionally examine your own self. You know you better than any other person knows you.

Realize that others will examine you.

"Who, when they had examined me, would have let me go, because there was no cause of death in me." Acts 28:18

"Mine answer to them that do examine me is this,"
1 Corinthians 9:3

Whether we like it or not, people will examine what we say and do. When this occurs, simply use it as another opportunity for you to objectively examine yourself and place the proper perspective upon the matter.

Focus

The third step to stay ReOrganized is to focus. Have the discipline to stay focused on the priorities in your life. That is, target your efforts; concentrate most of your attention on the priorities.

Part of staying focused, is to strip away all of the minor distractions which do not positively contribute to any of your priorities.

ReOrganizing Your Life comes through targeting your efforts. This is where the true test of discipline is seen in your life, that is, the ability to stay focused on the priorities you have set for your life.

People often lose their focus too easily. In this 21st Century, fast paced way of life, the art of being able to stay focused on the essential matters of one's life is quickly over shadowed by competing alternatives.

Having the discipline to stay focused will make it easier for you to pursue and manage your vision for your life.

Pursue

The fourth step to stay ReOrganized is to pursue. Be assertive enough to pursue what you have your focus on in life. That is, go after, follow through, and put into practice your priorities first.

"Depart from evil, and do good; seek peace, and pursue it."

Psalms 34:14

The word pursue, implies some form of movement or action taken in the direction of what is being pursued.

The Webster's 1828 Dictionary states, in part, that pursue means:

"1. To follow; to go or proceed after or in a like direction.
2. To take and proceed in, without following another.
3. To follow with a view to overtake; to follow with haste; to chase;
4. To seek; to use measures to obtain;
5. To prosecute; to continue.
6. To follow as an example; to imitate.
7. To endeavor to attain to; to strive to reach or gain." [48]

"Finally, brethren, whatsoever things are true, whatsoever things are honest, whatsoever things are just, whatsoever things are pure, whatsoever things are lovely, whatsoever things are of good report; if there be any virtue, and if there be any praise, think on these things." "Those things, which ye have both learned, and received, and heard, and seen in me, do: and the God of peace shall be with you." Philippians 4:8-9

"Go get it, simply go get it"; whatever it may be, as long as it is true, honest, just, pure, lovely and of good report, pursue it!

In other words, follow hard after your vision; make it an object of your desire, focusing constant efforts at achieving it. Hunt for it and chase it, if necessary.

ReOrganizing Your Life will, often, bring about new circumstances and situations which may compel us to pursue new methods and untried courses in order to accomplish changes.

Manage

The fifth step to stay ReOrganized is to manage.

Continually manage the affairs of your life; that is, stay in control of what is happening and be a good steward over your life.

Take dominion over your life. Part of taking dominion is to actively manage the affairs of your life. GOD gave mankind dominion upon the earth to dress and keep it (manage it).

> *"And God said, Let us make man in our image, after our likeness: and let them have dominion over the fish of the sea, and over the fowl of the air, and over the cattle, and over all the earth, and over every creeping thing that creepeth upon the earth." Genesis 1:26*

> *"And God blessed them, and God said unto them, Be fruitful, and multiply, and replenish the earth, and subdue it: and have dominion over the fish of the sea, and over the fowl of the air, and over every living thing that moveth upon the earth." Genesis 1:28*

> *"And the LORD God took the man, and put him into the garden of Eden to dress it and to keep it." Genesis 2:15*

To have dominion upon the earth requires that you first have dominion over your own life. This in turn, means that you must dress and keep, or manage your own life.

With the inherent responsibility of dominion comes the responsibility of stewardship.

There comes a time when we all must give an account of our stewardship and how faithfully we managed the affairs of our life.

> *"And he said also unto his disciples, There was a certain rich man, which had a steward; and the same was accused unto him that he had wasted his goods." "And he called him, and said unto him, How is it that I hear this of thee? give an account of thy stewardship; for thou mayest be no longer steward." "Then the steward said within himself, What shall I do? for my lord taketh away from me the stewardship: I cannot dig; to beg I am ashamed." "I am resolved what to do, that, when I am put out of the stewardship, they may receive me into their houses." Luke 16:1-4*

"And the Lord said, Who then is that faithful and wise steward, whom his lord shall make ruler over his household, to give them their portion of meat in due season?" Luke 12:42

Are you a faithful and wise steward over the affairs of your life? Can you be accused of wasting the goods entrusted to you? Well the question is, what will you do about it?

CHAPTER FIVE

ROYL Principles ™

Seven ROYL Principles:

1. To ReOrganize Your Life, have an effective and efficient way to stay ReOrganized.

2. To ReOrganize Your Life, allow the LORD to order your steps in life.

3. To ReOrganize Your Life, *prioritize* the important matters in your life.

4. To ReOrganize Your Life, take the necessary time to periodically *examine* your life.

5. To ReOrganize Your Life, have the discipline to *focus* on the priorities in your life.

6. To ReOrganize Your Life, be assertive enough to *pursue* what you have your focus on in life.

7. To ReOrganize Your Life, continually *manage* the affairs of your life.

CHAPTER SIX

True Meaning To The Power Of Organizing

By faith we understand that the worlds [during the successive ages] were framed (fashioned, *put in order*, and equipped for their intended purpose) by the word of God, so that what we see was not made out of things which are visible. Hebrews 11:3 AMP {Emphasis added}

CHAPTER SIX

True Meaning To The Power Of Organizing

At this point, it may go without saying that I believe order is at the very center or core of everything that GOD has done and does in all creation.

To begin with, let's return to the definition for reorganize, as stated in Chapter 2. <u>Reorganize</u>: *to organize again or anew*; to place in order again; return to order; to arrange again; *to bring order to again or anew*.

It was also stated in Chapter 2 that, "In the beginning of mankind, GOD, the Great ReOrganizer, first established or set forth order; as witnessed by the first chapter of the Book of Genesis. GOD started mankind by reorganizing life." Thus, I believe that the Bible is the primary resource to use to ReOrganize Your Life.

In Chapter 3, I said that "First, in order to ReOrganize Your Life, you must hold true to *your doctrine*." and that, "Your doctrine in life is a primary key to every other area in your life and will dictate how you live and how you ReOrganize Your Life."

In other words, the value of doctrine on how you handle life has great significance and power.

The Power Of Organizing

The very organism and structure in life itself is found in the Book of Genesis.

As I said earlier, in the beginning, GOD created the heaven and the earth. The earth was unformed, void and dark. Genesis Chapters One and Two of the Bible are foundation chapters of GOD's divine reorganization of the earth and life on the earth.

I believe that, within these two chapters of Genesis, GOD gave mankind foundation principles on how to reorganize anything on the earth, thus letting all things to be done decently and in order.

In the first chapters of the Book of Genesis, GOD reorganized life by setting forth foundational doctrine which can be used to ReOrganize Your Life. You will see that the elements and power for an organized way of life are found within the Book of Genesis.

The essence of every thing that mankind needed from the beginning to end for an organized and full life has its origin in Genesis. The Alpha and the Omega, for how to ReOrganize Your Life is JESUS CHRIST Himself.

As stated previously, in Chapter 3, "Your doctrine is the foundation for every decision you make in life, directly or indirectly; consciously or unconsciously. Your doctrine determines who you really are. Your doctrine in life determines what you do with your relationships, your resources, and your time."

Your doctrine, is a powerful source when it comes time for you to truly ReOrganize Your Life.

Having said that, the true meaning to the power of ReOrganzing Your Life is to have faith in and rely upon the power of GOD. Allow GOD to direct your life through His Word.

"That your faith should not stand in the wisdom of men, but in the power of God." 1 Corinthians 2:5

"According as his divine power hath given unto us all things that pertain unto life and godliness, through the knowledge of him that hath called us to glory and virtue:" 2 Peter 1:3

Again, let me reiterate, your doctrine is a powerful source when it comes time for you to truly ReOrganize Your Life.

Since doctrine is a powerful source in life, the Word of GOD is where our doctrine and power for life should begin and end.

"The Doctrinal Value of the First Chapters of Genesis" is described within a publication titled "The Fundamentals" and is stated in excerpts as follows:

"The Doctrinal Value of the First Chapters of Genesis"

"The Book of Genesis is in many respects the most important book in the Bible. It is of the first importance because it answers, not exhaustively, but sufficiently, the fundamental questions of the human mind. It contains the first authoritative information given to the race concerning these questions of everlasting interest:"

"Or, to put it in another way, the Book of Genesis is the seed in which the plant of God's Word is enfolded. It is the starting point of God's gradually unfolded plan of the ages. Genesis is the plinth of the pillar of the Divine revelation. It is the root of the tree of the inspired Scriptures. It is the source of the stream of the holy writings of the Bible."

"Further: in the first chapters of the Book of Genesis you have the strong and sufficient foundation of the subsequent developments of the kingdom of God; the root-germ of all ..."

"The Book of Genesis is the foundation on which the superstructure of the Scriptures rests. The foundation of the foundation is the first three chapters, which form in themselves a complete monograph of revelation. And of this final substructure the first three verses of the first chapter are the foundation."

"It is a narrative for mankind to show that this world was made by God for the habitation of man, and was gradually being fitted for God's children. So in a series of successive creative developments from the formless chaos, containing in embryonic condition all elemental constituents, chemical and mechanical, air, earth, fire, and water, the sublime process is recorded, according to the Genesis narrative in ... order:"

"Finally, we have in Genesis 2 the doctrinal foundation of those great fundamentals, the necessity of labor, the Lord's Day of rest, the

Divine ordinance of matrimony, and the home life of mankind. The weekly day of rest was provided for man by his God, and is planted in the very forefront of revelation as a Divine ordinance, and so also is marriage and the home. Our Lord Jesus Christ endorses the Mosaic story of the creation of Adam and Eve, refers to it as the explanation of the Divine will regarding divorce, and sanctions by His infallible imprimatur that most momentous of ethical questions, monogamy. Thus the great elements of life as God intended it, the three universal factors of happy, healthy, helpful life, law, labor, love, are laid down in the beginning of God's Book." {Emphasis added} [49]

Although this publication speaks more in depth on the value of biblical doctrinal matters, it is simply used here to emphasize the value, importance and power of doctrine when it comes time to ReOrganize Your Life™.

The major point is that, the Book of Genesis can be used to gain foundation and wisdom on ReOrganizing the many areas of our life.

So that I am not misleading and to avoid confusion, this is not to imply that every principle and comment mentioned in this book on ReOrganizing Your Life is considered to be "biblical doctrine". In certain cases, it is merely wisdom, principles or a framework drawn from and based upon the Bible and "biblical doctrine".

It is by having faith in GOD that we can put true meaning to the power of order in our life. We can frame our lives according to the standards of the Word of GOD.

> *"Through faith we understand that the worlds were **framed** by the word of God, so that things which are seen were not made of things which do appear." Hebrews 11:3 {Emphasis added}*

> *"By faith we understand that the worlds [during the successive ages] were **framed** (**fashioned, put in order**, and equipped for their intended purpose) by the word of God, so that what we see was not made out of things which are visible." Hebrews 11:3 AMP {Emphasis added}*

By now you have become accustomed to, and have realized, by reading this book that I prefer to bring true meaning to matters by offering definitions for certain words. So let me define the word "frame".

According to Webster's 1828 Dictionary the words frame and framed has the following meaning:

"Frame:
1. To fit or prepare and unite several parts in a regular structure or entire thing; to fabricate by orderly construction and union of various parts; as, to frame a house or other building.
2. To fit one thing to another; to adjust; to make suitable.
3. To make; to compose; as, to frame a law...
4. To regulate; to adjust; to shape; to conform; as, to frame our lives according to the rules of the gospel."

"Framed:
Fitted and united in due form; made; composed; devised; adjusted." [50]

Framed, as used in Hebrews 11:3, is the Greek word "2675, katartizo (kat-ar-tid'-zo)" which means "to complete thoroughly, i.e. repair (literally or figuratively) or adjust:—fit, frame, mend, (make) perfect(-ly join together), prepare, restore." [51]

Considering the above, I believe it is fair to say that the implication, in Hebrews Chapter 11 verse 3, is that GOD organized or ReOrganized the worlds. He ordered the ages and thus the life contained there in.

All matter, visible and invisible was fitted and united in due form, made, composed, devised and adjusted by GOD. It was framed by GOD.

And it is through faith that we must understand that the worlds were repaired, joined together, restored, set in order or [organized] by GOD.

To further our understanding of this, however, consider what others have said:

"Were framed; It is observable that the apostle does not here use the word *make or create*. That which he does use —katartizo— means, to put in order, to arrange, to complete, and may be applied to that which before had an existence, and which is to be put in order or re-fitted, Mt 4:24; Mr 1:19; Mt 21:16; Heb 10:5. The meaning here is, that they *were set in order* by the word of God. This implies the act of creation, but the specific idea is that of *arranging* them in the beautiful order in which they are now."—Albert Barnes' Notes on the Bible [52]

"Were framed by the word of God; heaven, earth, and seas, with all their hosts of creatures, the visible creation and the invisible world, were put into being and existence, placed in their proper order, disposed and fitted to their end, by the mighty word of God:"—Matthew Poole's Commentary on the Holy Bible [53]

"By faith we understand that the worlds - Heaven and earth and all things in them, visible and invisible. [W]ere made—Formed, fashioned, and finished. By the word—The sole command of God,"—John Wesley's Notes on the Bible [54]

To reiterate, through faith we understand that matters were organized and ReOrganized by the Word of GOD.

You can use the Word of GOD to ReOrganize Your Life™. You can bring true meaning to the power of organizing by reading, studying and implementing the principles and standards contained in the Bible.

The Bible is a book about life. It is the Book on how to receive true meaning to life. The Bible is the Book about the greatest life ever lived. It is the Book about the life of JESUS CHRIST, LORD and SAVIOUR of mankind in the world.

The Bible says:

"And ye shall know the truth, and the truth shall make you free." John 8:32

The Book of Genesis is all about truth; it is about JESUS CHRIST, who is "the way, the truth and the life." (John 14:6)

JESUS CHRIST, the One who came, gave His life and was resurrected for the purpose of ReOrganizing Your Life.

Therefore, as stated previously, I believe that the Book of Genesis is the standard by which you can use to ReOrganize Your Life.

The Genesis Standard is a model of the Genesis of Organizing; it is a model or standard of how to ReOrganize Your Life.

The Genesis of Organizing

"Genesis is a name taken from the Greek, and signifies "the book of generation or production;" it is properly so called, as containing an account of the origin of all things." — Matthew Henry's Concise Commentary [55]

Genesis is the beginning of everything, including life itself, for mankind.

In the Genesis of Organizing, GOD performed different activities and accomplished different things at different times. He did not try to do everything at one time. Instead, GOD divided the tasks of creation into six major stages to complete.

GOD decided to take six days to ReOrganize life. GOD, being GOD, could have completed everything in one day or one hour, but He organized the task of Creation into six stages to accomplish the overall goal of ReOrganizing life. In doing so, He established a standard or model in the process.

By reading and understanding the Book of Genesis we can see that it is, generally, divided into two basic segments, the first, which is about the Order of Creation and the second, which is primarily about ReOrganizing the life created.

Let us briefly, examine the Order of Creation;

"First day: making light and dividing it from darkness. Ge 1:3-5; 2 Co 4:6

Second day: making the firmament or atmosphere, and separating the waters. Ge 1:6-8

Third day: separating the land from the water, and making it fruitful. Ge 1:9-13

Fourth day: placing the sun, moon, and stars to give light, Ge 1:14-19

Fifth day: making birds, insects, and fishes. Ge 1:20-23

Sixth day: making beasts of the earth, and man. Ge 1:24,28

God rested, on the seventh day. Ge 2:2-3"—Torrey's Topical Textbook [56]

*"By faith we understand that the worlds [during the successive ages] were **framed (fashioned, put in order**, and equipped for their intended purpose) by the word of God, so that what we see was not made out of things which are visible." Hebrews 11:3 AMP {Emphasis added}*

"Moreover, Genesis alone describes creation out of nothing, as distinguished from creation out of preexisting materials.

Genesis alone recognizes the law of progress in creation: first light, then order, then life, vegetable, grass, herb, fruit tree; then animal life… Also progressive advance in life: (1) aquatic animals and fish; (2) fowl; (3) terrestrial animals; (4) man, the apex of creation. The advance is orderly, from the lower to the higher organizations."—Fausset's Bible Dictionary [57]

Genesis is a Book of order. It is the Genesis of Organizing and ReOrganzing life. GOD framed or ordered everything by His Word.

"These are the generations of the heavens and of the earth when they were created, in the day that the LORD God made the earth and the heavens," Genesis 2:4

GOD ordered everything by His Word, in doing so, I believe that GOD, also indirectly, created and made a standard or model in the Book of Genesis that can be used for ReOrganizing our lives.

The Genesis Standard of ReOrganizing

To ReOrganize Your Life™, you may need to consider and apply, what I call the Genesis Standard of ReOrganizing.

First, let's define what a standard is.

Standard:
"2. That which is established by sovereign power as a rule or measure by which others are to be adjusted... 3. That which is established as a rule or model, by the authority of public opinion, or by respectable opinions, or by custom or general consent; ..." [58]

GOD established His doctrine in the Word of GOD to be a standard for living life in the earth.

Within the Book of Genesis, and indeed throughout the Bible, GOD established certain standards for man to live by.

As an example, here are two:

A standard for Adam about the tree of the knowledge of good and evil:

"And the LORD God commanded the man, saying, Of every tree of the garden thou mayest freely eat: But of the tree of the knowledge of good and evil, thou shalt not eat of it: for in the day that thou eatest thereof thou shalt surely die."
Genesis 2:16-17

The standard for man Adam was that, of every tree of the garden he could freely eat. But man Adam could not freely eat of the tree of the knowledge of good and evil.

A standard for when a man has a wife (woman):

"And the LORD God said, It is not good that the man should be alone; I will make him an help meet for him. And Adam said, This is now bone of my bones, and flesh of my flesh: she shall be called Woman, because she was taken out of

Man. Therefore shall a man leave his father and his mother, and shall cleave unto his wife: and they shall be one flesh." Genesis 2:18, 23-24

The standard was that a man shall leave his father and mother, cleave to his wife and become one flesh.

GOD, through His Word, has given different models; ordinances, laws, commandments, statues, rules, and direction, in general, which could be considered standards.

In other words, GOD established by His Sovereign power, rules or measures by which we can adjust or ReOrganize our lives.

I want to say again, so that I am very clear and not misleading, this is not to say that everything in this book on ReOrganizing Your Life is intended to be "doctrine" from the Word of GOD. But, is simply a standard or model for how you can ReOrganize Your Life™.

One of the most important things that we can learn from the Word of GOD in Genesis chapter one and the beginning of Genesis chapter two, on how to ReOrganize Your Life is, do not try to do it all in one day. Avoid trying to do it all in one day.

As we have noted previously, the complete vision of GOD for ReOrganizing was a Seven Day plan. This is significant, because it is commonly understood that the number seven symbolizes perfection or completion.

It may or may not be a seven day plan of completion for you, but the main point is, do not try to do it all in one day. Take the necessary amount of time to complete your vision.

Now, what follows is what I call The Genesis Standard for ReOrganizing Your Life. It is a model which consists of ten general components to consider when ReOrganizing. These ten components can be used as a general model to help you ReOrganize any area of your life.

It is not by coincidence, but with clear intent that my focus here is on ten components, and not some other number, since "ten denotes the perfection of Divine order. But this Divine order implies responsibility for man, and so ten denotes man's responsibility toward God." "In Genesis 1 the words "God said" occur ten times, speaking of man's responsibility in the presence of God's Word" [59]

The bottom line is that, although we have GOD's Divine order at work for us, we have a personal responsibility toward GOD for how we choose to live our life, rather ReOrganized or disorganized.

The Genesis Standard For ReOrganizing Your Life

Standard # 1: **Acknowledge**
You must acknowledge the current conditions of disorder in your life.

One of the first things you must do is acknowledge your current conditions in the area of life needing ReOrganized.

> *"And the earth was without form, and void; and darkness was upon the face of the deep.* And the Spirit of God moved upon the face of the waters."
> Genesis 1:2 {Emphasis added}

Prior to doing anything about ReOrganizing, GOD acknowledged the current conditions. He acknowledged that the earth was without form, void and dark or as I say disorganized (refer back to Chapter two of this book).

Acknowledge means:
"1. To own, avow or admit to be true, by a declaration of assent;
...
2. To own or notice with particular regard.
3. To own or confess, as implying a consciousness of guilt."
[60]

Take ownership of the disorder in your life, admit it to be a true fact.
You must be honest and truthful with yourself and acknowledge that you are disorganized in a certain area of life. And then, you must desire to do what it takes to make the appropriate changes or adjust-

ments. (Please review the first five Chapters of this book on how to go about this in more detail).

Standard # 2: **Move**
You must move upon the current conditions of disorder.

You move upon the conditions by taking action in the area needing to be ReOrganized.

*"And the earth was without form, and void; and darkness was upon the face of the deep. **And the Spirit of God moved upon the face of the waters.**" Genesis 1:2 {Emphasis added}*

After GOD acknowledged the current conditions He moved upon the conditions. He took action to ReOrganize the earth.
You too, must move upon the conditions in your life to ReOrganize Your Life. Take action now.

Move means:
"1. To impel; to carry, convey or draw from one place to another; to cause to change place or posture in any manner or by any means...
2. To excite into action; to affect; to agitate;
3. To cause to act or determine; as, to move the will.
4. To persuade; to prevail on; to excite from a state of rest or indifference." [61]

You must have a cause to act and change from a state of rest or indifference on the disorder in your life.
Realize that there is a reason for you to move upon the condition.
We often accept the disorder by remaining inactive toward the condition. You must see that, that is not enough to acknowledge the disorder, you must also move upon it.
The operative word here is move (act), do not just sit idle doing nothing about the disorder. (Please refer to Chapters four and five of this book for additional information).

Standard # 3: **Say**
You must say what specific condition you want to exist.

You must say by speaking about what it is that you want to exist.

"And God **said**, Let there be light: and there was light."

"And God **said**, Let there be a firmament in the midst of the waters, and let it divide the waters from the waters."

"And God **said**, Let the waters under the heaven be gathered together unto one place, and let the dry land appear: and it was so."

"And God **said**, Let the earth bring forth grass, the herb yielding seed, and the fruit tree yielding fruit after his kind, whose seed is in itself, upon the earth: and it was so."

"And God **said**, Let there be lights in the firmament of the heaven to divide the day from the night; and let them be for signs, and for seasons, and for days, and years:"

"And God **said**, Let the waters bring forth abundantly the moving creature that hath life, and fowl that may fly above the earth in the open firmament of heaven."

"And God **said**, Let the earth bring forth the living creature after his kind, cattle, and creeping thing, and beast of the earth after his kind: and it was so."

"And God **said**, Let us make man in our image, after our likeness: and let them have dominion over the fish of the sea, and over the fowl of the air, and over the cattle, and over all the earth, and over every creeping thing that creepeth upon the earth."

"And God blessed them, and God **said** unto them, Be fruit-

ful, and multiply, and replenish the earth, and subdue it: and have dominion over the fish of the sea, and over the fowl of the air, and over every living thing that moveth upon the earth."

*"And God **said**, Behold, I have given you every herb bearing seed, which is upon the face of all the earth, and every tree, in the which is the fruit of a tree yielding seed; to you it shall be for meat." Genesis 1:3, 6, 9, 11, 14, 20, 24, 26, 28, 29 {Emphasis added}*

After acknowledging and moving upon, next, GOD said what specific condition He wanted to exist for each area.

In Genesis Chapter One, GOD "said" ten separate times as he moved upon the conditions.

You too, must begin to specifically say what it is that you are going to do about your current conditions. Begin to vocalize what you intend to do about the disorder. Say what your vision is for that particular area of your life.

Said means:
1. Declared; uttered; reported.
2. Aforesaid; before mentioned." [62]

As GOD said, "it was so" (Genesis 1:3, 9, 11 and 20). GOD first said it and then it was so. Before the earth was actually ReOrganized, HE declared it so.

Declare, utter and report what it is that you desire to ReOrganize. Get a vision. (Please refer to Chapter four of this book for more detail)

Standard # 4: **Let**
You must let the condition that you want, to exist.

You must mentally and physically allow the new condition or order to exist before it can become a reality.

GOD permitted or allowed that specific condition HE said to exist.

GOD said "let" fourteen times in Genesis Chapter One. The word let is a word which implies permission. It is a word that denotes a permissive action or allows something to transpire.

*"And God said, **Let** there be light: and there was light."*

*"And God said, **Let** there be a firmament in the midst of the waters, and **let** it divide the waters from the waters."*

*"And God said, **Let** the waters under the heaven be gathered together unto one place, and **let** the dry land appear: and it was so."*

*"And God said, **Let** the earth bring forth grass, the herb yielding seed, and the fruit tree yielding fruit after his kind, whose seed is in itself, upon the earth: and it was so."*

*"And God said, **Let** there be lights in the firmament of the heaven to divide the day from the night; and **let** them be for signs, and for seasons, and for days, and years:"*

*"And **let** them be for lights in the firmament of the heaven to give light upon the earth: and it was so."*

*"And God said, **Let** the waters bring forth abundantly the moving creature that hath life, and fowl that may fly above the earth in the open firmament of heaven."*

*"And God blessed them, saying, Be fruitful, and multiply, and fill the waters in the seas, and **let** fowl multiply in the earth."*

*"And God said, **Let** the earth bring forth the living creature after his kind, cattle, and creeping thing, and beast of the earth after his kind: and it was so."*

*"And God said, **Let** us make man in our image, after our*

*likeness: and **let** them have dominion over the fish of the sea, and over the fowl of the air, and over the cattle, and over all the earth, and over every creeping thing that creepeth upon the earth." Genesis 1:3, 6, 9, 11, 14, 15, 20, 22, 24, 26 {Emphasis added}*

Let means:
"1. To permit; to allow; to suffer; to give leave or power by a positive act, or negatively, to withhold restraint; not to prevent." [63]

By acknowledging, moving upon and saying, you then will be able to permit or allow a new condition to happen or exist. You allow it to be so.

So far we see the foundation phases of ReOrganizing, GOD first acknowledged, next moved upon, followed by saying and letting, then it was so.

[Acknowledge + Move upon + Say + Let = It was so]

The four components of the Standard make up the primary components for the Genesis of Organizing. These four components are the building blocks or pavement on which ReOrganizing takes form.

This, as I see it, is a summary of what you can do to get started on the road toward ReOrganizing Your Life.

The next five components of the Standard which follow, are what I call, the framework and walls of ReOrganizing.

Standard # 5: **See**
You must see that what you want is good.

You must be able to see that your vision for ReOrganizing is a good one.

*"And God **saw** the light, that it was good: and God divided the light from the darkness."*

*"And God called the dry land Earth; and the gathering together of the waters called he Seas: and God **saw** that it was good."*

*"And the earth brought forth grass, and herb yielding seed after his kind, and the tree yielding fruit, whose seed was in itself, after his kind: and God **saw** that it was good."*

*"And to rule over the day and over the night, and to divide the light from the darkness: and God **saw** that it was good."*

*"And God created great whales, and every living creature that moveth, which the waters brought forth abundantly, after their kind, and every winged fowl after his kind: and God **saw** that it was good."*

*"And God made the beast of the earth after his kind, and cattle after their kind, and every thing that creepeth upon the earth after his kind: and God **saw** that it was good."*

*"And God **saw** every thing that he had made, and, behold, it was very good. And the evening and the morning were the sixth day." Genesis 1:4, 10, 12, 18, 21, 25, 31 {Emphasis added}*

See means:
"1. To perceive by the eye; to have knowledge of the existence and the apparent qualities of objects by the organs of sight; to behold.
2. To observe; to note or notice; to know; to regard or look to; to take care; to attend, as to the execution of some order, or to the performance of something." [64]

GOD was able to see or perceive that everything He made was good.

You too, must begin to perceive and observe that the new change of order is good for your life. It must be something that you wholeheartedly desire.

If you do not see or perceive that ReOrganizing is good, then it will not be sustained by you for any significant length of time.

Standard # 6: **Call**
You must call your new order in life something.

Calling or labeling your new order in life gives it an identity. Its identity will let it become more of a reality within your mind.
You must give your ReOrganizing project a label, name it.

*"And God **called** the light Day, and the darkness he **called** Night. And the evening and the morning were the first day."*

*"And God **called** the firmament Heaven. And the evening and the morning were the second day."*

*"And God **called** the dry land Earth; and the gathering together of the waters **called** he Seas: and God saw that it was good." Genesis 1:5, 8, 10 {Emphasis added}*

Call means:
"1. To name; to denominate or give a name. And God called the light day, and the darkness he called night. Gen. 1...
6. To give notice to come by authority; to command to come; as, call a servant.
7. To proclaim; to name, or publish the name." [65]

Name or proclaim and give notice to what you are doing and have done. Publish it, even if it is only to you. By this, I do not refer to or mean the charismatic teaching of "name it and claim".
Calling or labeling simply gives an identity to what you are doing.

Standard # 7: **Create or Make**
You must create or make what you want.

When you cannot find exactly what you want, you must get creative and make it out of what exists.

"In the beginning God **created** the heaven and the earth."

"And God **created** great whales, and every living creature that moveth, which the waters brought forth abundantly, after their kind, and every winged fowl after his kind: and God saw that it was good."

"So God **created** man in his own image, in the image of God **created** he him; male and female **created** he them."

"And God blessed the seventh day, and sanctified it: because that in it he had rested from all his work which God **created** and made."

"These are the generations of the heavens and of the earth when they were **created**, in the day that the LORD God made the earth and the heavens," Genesis 1:7, 16, 25, 26, 31; 2:2, 3, 4 {Emphasis added}

"And God **made** the firmament, and divided the waters which were under the firmament from the waters which were above the firmament: and it was so."

"And God **made** two great lights; the greater light to rule the day, and the lesser light to rule the night: he **made** the stars also."

"And God **made** the beast of the earth after his kind, and cattle after their kind, and every thing that creepeth upon the earth after his kind: and God saw that it was good."

"And God said, Let us **make** man in our image, after our likeness: and let them have dominion over the fish of the sea, and over the fowl of the air, and over the cattle, and over all the earth, and over every creeping thing that creepeth upon the earth."

*"And God saw every thing that he had **made**, and, behold, it was very good. And the evening and the morning were the sixth day."*

*"And on the seventh day God ended his work which he had **made**; and he rested on the seventh day from all his work which he had **made**."*

*"And God blessed the seventh day, and sanctified it: because that in it he had rested from all his work which God created and **made**."*

*"These are the generations of the heavens and of the earth when they were created, in the day that the LORD God **made** the earth and the heavens," Genesis 1:1, 21, 27; 2:3, 4 {Emphasis added}*

"Create:
1. To produce; to bring into being from nothing; to cause to exist. In the beginning, God created the heaven and the earth. Genesis 1"
"3. To produce; to cause; to be the occasion of.
4. To beget; to generate; to bring forth.
5. To make or produce, by new combinations of matter already created, and by investing these combinations with new forms, constitutions and qualities; to shape and **organize**. God created man in his own image. Genesis 1.
6. To form anew; to change the state or character; to renew."
[66] {Emphasis added}

"Gen 1:1-**Create**:
254. Bara'; to create, form, make, produce; to cut, to cut down; to engrave, to carve. This word occurs in the very first verse of the Bible (Gen. 1:1). Bara' emphasizes the initiation of the object, not manipulating it after original creation. The word as used…refers only to an activity which can be performed by God. Entirely new productions are associated with bara'… The word also possesses the meaning of

'bringing into existence"... Therefore, it is not surprising that it is used in Gen. 1:1, 21, 27; 2:3. There is every reason to believe that bara' was creation ex nihilo (out of nothing)." [67]

Make means:
> "2. To form of materials; to fashion; to mold into shape; to cause to exist in a different form, or as a distinct thing. God not only made, but created; not only made the work, but the materials.
> 3. To create; to cause to exist; to form from nothing. God made the materials of the earth and of all worlds.
> 4. To compose; to constitute as parts, materials or ingredients united in a whole. These several sums make the whole amount. The heaven, the air, the earth, and boundless sea," [68]

"Gen 1:16-Made: Gen 1:26-Make:
6213. 'Asah; this important root means to work, labor, toil; to make, create, construct, build; to accomplish; to acquire, earn, procure; to prepare; to offer, sacrifice; to appoint; to constitute; to keep; to fulfill; to happen; to be; to handle; to squeeze. The basic meaning of 'asah is "do" or "make" in a general sense... In the account of creation, bara' (1254) and 'asah alternate. Bara' conveys the thought of creation ex nihilo (out of nothing), while 'asah is broader in scope and dealt with refinement. In other words, the emphasis was on fashioning the created objects..." [69]

You must sometimes work or fashion things out of what exists.

The two words, create and make, are used here as in Genesis to point out that sometimes we can simply take what exists and ReOrganize. But then, there are times that it may require you get creative and make or produce new combinations to ReOrganize the condition in your life.

Standard # 8: **Set**
You must sometimes set some things in place.

You must, on occasion, deliberately or purposely, set or put matters in its proper place in your life.

*"And God **set** them in the firmament of the heaven to give light upon the earth," Genesis 1:17 {Emphasis added}*

Set means:
"...to dispose or **put in order**, to establish, found or institute, to possess, to cease;
1. To put or place; to fix or cause to rest in a standing posture.
2. To put or place in its proper or natural posture.
3. To put, place or fix in any situation. God set the sun, moon and stars in the firmament.
4. To put into any condition or state.
5. To put; to fix; to attach to." [70] {Emphasis added}

GOD made and then, deliberately with purpose, set the lights in the firmament of the heaven.

Take the necessary time and make the effort to set the areas of your life in proper order. Give light to your ReOrganized life.

Standard # 9: **Divide and Gather**
You must sometimes divide and gather some things.

At times you may need to divide or separate certain things or areas within your life in order to get better control of your life.

Then, at times you may need to gather together certain things or areas within your life in order to get better control of your life.

*"And God saw the light, that it was good: and God **divided** the light from the darkness."*

*"And God said, Let there be a firmament in the midst of the waters, and let it **divide** the waters from the waters."*

*"And God made the firmament, and **divided** the waters which were under the firmament from the waters which were above*

the firmament: and it was so."

*"And God said, Let there be lights in the firmament of the heaven to **divide** the day from the night; and let them be for signs, and for seasons, and for days, and years:"*

*"And to rule over the day and over the night, and to **divide** the light from the darkness: and God saw that it was good." Genesis 1:4, 6, 7, 14, 18 [Emphasis added]*

*"And God said, Let the waters under the heaven be **gathered** together unto one place, and let the dry land appear: and it was so." Genesis 1:9 [Emphasis added]*

Divide means:
"1. To part or separate an entire thing; to part a thing into two or more pieces.
2. To cause to be separate; to keep apart by a partition or by an imaginary line or limit. Let the firmament divide the waters from the waters. Genesis 1.
3. To make partition of, among a number.
4. To open; to cleave." [71]

Gather means:
"1. To bring together; to collect a number of separate things into one place or into one aggregate body.
7. To select and take; to separate from others and bring together. [72]

GOD divided or gathered certain things to give them their own distinct purpose in the greater scheme of things.

In ReOrganizing Your Life, you too must make certain decisions on when to divide and gather together certain things or areas within your life.

The last component for the Genesis Standard is the finished component of ReOrganizing.

Standard # 10: **Bless and Rest**
You must take the time to bless and rest when finished.

You must bless what you have done and then rest. Rest and enjoy the good of what you have ReOrganized.

*"And God **blessed** them, saying, Be fruitful, and multiply, and fill the waters in the seas, and let fowl multiply in the earth."*

*"And God **blessed** them, and God said unto them, Be fruitful, and multiply, and replenish the earth, and subdue it: and have dominion over the fish of the sea, and over the fowl of the air, and over every living thing that moveth upon the earth."*

*"And on the seventh day God ended his work which he had made; and he **rested** on the seventh day from all his work which he had made."*

*"And God **blessed** the seventh day, and sanctified it: because that in it he had **rested** from all his work which God created and made." Genesis 1:22, 28; 2:2, 3 [Emphasis added]*

Bless means:
"1. To pronounce a wish of happiness to one; to express a wish or desire of happiness.
2. To make happy; to make successful; to prosper in temporal concerns; as, we are blest with peace and plenty.
3. To make happy in a future life.
4. To set apart or consecrate to holy purposes; to make and pronounce holy.

And God blessed the seventh day and sanctified it. Gen. 2

5. To consecrate by prayer; to invoke a blessing upon."
[73]

Rest means:

"1. Cessation of motion or action of any kind, and applicable to any body or being; as rest from labor; rest from mental exertion; rest of body or mind. A body is at rest, when it ceases to move; the mind is at rest, when it ceases to be disturbed or agitated; the sea is never at rest. Hence,
2. Quiet; repose; a state free from motion or disturbance; a state of reconciliation to God.

Learn of me, for I am meek and lowly in heart; and ye shall find rest to your souls." Matt.11. [74]

Rest:
"7673. shabath (*shaw-bath'*) Hebrew;a primitive root; to repose, i.e. desist from exertion; used in many implied relations—(cause to, let, make to) cease, celebrate, cause (make) to fail, keep (sabbath), suffer to be lacking, leave, put away (down)..." [75]

Recognize or set apart what you have finished and be happy about it.

When GOD ended or finished His ReOrganizing work He rested.

You, too, need to take the time to rest. Cease from the activity and enjoy it, celebrate before moving on to another area to ReOrganize Your Life.

GOD made and created you in His image, so you too can have the power to ReOrganize Your Life.

"And God said, Let us make man in our image, after our likeness: and let them have dominion over the fish of the sea, and over the fowl of the air, and over the cattle, and over all the earth, and over every creeping thing that creepeth upon the earth." "So God created man in his own image, in the image of God created he him; male and female created he them." "And God blessed them, and God said unto them, Be fruitful, and multiply, and replenish the earth, and subdue it: and have dominion over the fish of the sea, and over the fowl

of the air, and over every living thing that moveth upon the earth." Genesis 1:26-28

It will take order, to have dominion, be fruitful, multiply, replenish and subdue.

The Genesis Standard for ReOrganizing is not just some theory on order, but an actual practical principle and guide to help you ReOrganize Your Life™. I have applied the Genesis Standard most of my life.

The difference is, that only until I began to read, meditate and study the Word of GOD as it pertains to ReOrganizing, did I realize that I actually used the biblical principle of ReOrganizing. This is what I now call the Genesis Standard for how to ReOrganize Your Life™.

CHAPTER SIX

ROYL Principles ™

Seven ROYL Principles:

1. To ReOrganize Your Life, understand the value of doctrine.

2. To ReOrganize Your Life, have faith in and rely upon the power of GOD.

3. To ReOrganize Your Life, frame your life according to the standards of the Word of GOD.

4. To ReOrganize Your Life, bring true meaning to the power of organizing.

5. To ReOrganize Your Life, avoid trying to do it all in one day.

6. To ReOrganize Your Life, take ownership of the disorder in your life.

7. To ReOrganize Your Life, apply the Genesis Standard For ReOrganizing Your Life.

CHAPTER SEVEN

ROYL For CHRIST

"Of the increase of his government and peace there shall be no end, upon the throne of David, and upon his kingdom, *to order it*, and to establish it with judgment and with justice from henceforth even for ever. The zeal of the LORD of hosts will perform this." Isaiah 9:6-7 {Emphasis added}

CHAPTER SEVEN

ROYL For CHRIST

ROYL (pronounced royal) means ReOrganize Your Life. ROYL for CHRIST; ReOrganize Your Life for CHRIST. ROYL for JESUS CHRIST, the message is that ReOrganizing Your Life can only be complete in JESUS CHRIST.

Become a royal priesthood for CHRIST. Choose to ReOrganize Your Life and come out of the spiritual darkness and into the true light.

> *"But ye are a chosen generation, a royal priesthood, an holy nation, a peculiar people; that ye should shew forth the praises of him who hath called you out of darkness into his marvellous light:" 1Peter 2:9*

You can do every thing to ReOrganize in every area of life, but if you do not ROYL for CHRIST it will not be complete. Your life will always seem as though something is missing and, indeed, there is.

ROYL For CHRIST First

JESUS CHRIST needs to be the first in order, when it comes to ReOrganizing Your Life.

"But every man in his own order: Christ the firstfruits; afterward they that are Christ's at his coming." 1Corinthians 15:23

Although the context of the above verse is in reference to death and resurrection, it is used here to emphasize the life which is ordered in CHRIST.

Every person in their own order, but CHRIST will be the first of fruits in a completed life. This is how it will be like it or not, in the end when this life is finished.

But you may be thinking, what is a first-fruit? Well I am glad that you are thinking that.

First-fruits:
"1. The fruit or produce first matured and collected in any season...
2. The first profits of any thing..." [76]

First-fruits are the first of the fruits of the season which come to maturity and thus can be used for profit first, in order.

"But every man in his own order—rather, "rank": the *Greek* is not in the abstract, but concrete: image from troops, "each in his own regiment." Though all shall rise again, let not any think all shall be saved; nay, each shall have his proper place, **Christ first (Col 1:18), and after Him the godly who die in Christ (1Th 4:16), in a separate band from the ungodly**, and then "the end," that is, the resurrection of the rest of the dead..." "**Christ's own flock shall share His glory "at His coming** ..." "... only the glory of them "that are Christ's," "... their personal union with Him as *their "Life" (Col 3:4)*..." [77] *Jamieson-Fausset-Brown Commentary* {Emphasis added}

*"When **Christ, who is our life**, shall appear, then shall ye also appear with him in glory." Colossians 3:4 {Emphasis added}*

CHRIST should be our life. For in him we should live, and move, and have our being (Acts 17:28).

There will not be an appearance by you with Him in glory, unless you ROYL for CHRIST.

> *"If ye then be risen with Christ, seek those things which are above, where Christ sitteth on the right hand of God." "Set your affection on things above, not on things on the earth." "For ye are dead, and your life is hid with Christ in God." "When Christ, who is our life, shall appear, then shall ye also appear with him in glory." Colossians 3:1-4*

We must die spiritually from this earthly life and be spiritually born again, if we are to be risen eternally with CHRIST, who died for our sins.

This means that you must ReOrganize Your Life for CHRIST. ROYL for CHRIST, by seeking those things which are above, where CHRIST sits on the right hand of GOD; set your affection on things above, not on things on the earth.

JESUS CHRIST was born of a virgin, died, has risen and will return to order the government of His Kingdom.

> *"For unto us a child is born, unto us a son is given: and the government shall be upon his shoulder: and his name shall be called Wonderful, Counselor, The mighty God, The everlasting Father, The Prince of Peace." "Of the increase of his government and peace there shall be no end, upon the throne of David, and upon his kingdom,* **to order it***, and to establish it with judgment and with justice from henceforth even for ever. The zeal of the LORD of hosts will perform this." Isaiah 9:6-7 {Emphasis added}*

The above verses from the Book of Isaiah are, as generally said; scripture from the Old Testament concealed and the verses, below, from the Book of Luke are scripture from the New Testament revealed. The New Testament reveals what is concealed in the Old Testament—in this case, it reveals who is being referenced, as well as other details and information.

> *"And in the sixth month the angel Gabriel was sent from God unto a city of Galilee, named Nazareth," "To a virgin espoused to a man whose name was Joseph, of the house of David; and the virgin's name was Mary." Luke 1:26-27*

> *"And the angel said unto her, Fear not, Mary: for thou hast found favour with God." "And, behold, thou shalt conceive in thy womb, and bring forth a son, and shalt call his name JESUS." "He shall be great, and shall be called the Son of the Highest: and the Lord God shall give unto him the throne of his father David:" "And he shall reign over the house of Jacob for ever; and of his kingdom there shall be no end." "Then said Mary unto the angel, How shall this be, seeing I know not a man?" "And the angel answered and said unto her, The Holy Ghost shall come upon thee, and the power of the Highest shall overshadow thee: therefore also that holy thing which shall be born of thee shall be called the Son of God." Luke 1:30-35*

JESUS CHRIST, the Son of GOD, will truly come to organize. He will order and establish His Kingdom, with judgment (His law) and justice (His righteousness); thus, there will be no end to His government and peace.

Are you prepared for eternity? If not, then you need to begin your preparation.

Your preparation for this awesome, majestic and holy event should take place while the choice is yours to make.

You can do something, now, to ReOrganize Your Life for the return of the LORD our GOD, JESUS CHRIST; ROYL for CHRIST.

In Chapter Three of this Book I mentioned that there were four basic areas when it comes to ReOrganizing Your Life; our doctrine, our relationships, our resources and our time. Begin by ReOrganizing Your Life for CHRIST in these four areas. If you allow Him to be first in these four areas, your life will be ReOrganized for eternity.

I personally believe that throughout eternity there will still be doctrine, relationships, resources and time; however, maybe not as we now understand it.

Why and How?

Why and how, should you ROYL for CHRIST? The answer is really quite simple. Why?—because He is GOD. How?—it is done by receiving His WORD.

GOD sent His WORD to ReOrganize Your Life.

"In the beginning was the Word, and the Word was with God, and the Word was God." "The same was in the beginning with God." "All things were made by him; and without him was not any thing made that was made." "In him was life; and the life was the light of men." John 1:1-4

All that we must do, is to receive life eternal, the light of men; that life and light is JESUS CHRIST.

"But as many as received him, to them gave he power to become the sons of God, even to them that believe on his name:" "Which were born, not of blood, nor of the will of the flesh, nor of the will of man, but of God." "And the Word was made flesh, and dwelt among us, (and we beheld his glory, the glory as of the only begotten of the Father,) full of grace and truth." John 1:12-14

The WORD of GOD (JESUS CHRIST) was made flesh, born of a virgin. He is the KING of Kings and LORD of Lords.

"And he was clothed with a vesture dipped in blood: and his name is called The Word of God." "And he hath on his vesture and on his thigh a name written, KING OF KINGS, AND LORD OF LORDS." Revelation 19:13, 16

GOD gave us His WORD, His only begotten SON.

> *"For God so loved the world, that he gave his only begotten Son, that whosoever believeth in him should not perish, but have everlasting life." "For God sent not his Son into the world to condemn the world; but that the world through him might be saved." "He that believeth on him is not condemned: but he that believeth not is condemned already, because he hath not believed in the name of the only begotten Son of God." John 3: 16-18*

GOD also gave us the HOLY SPIRIT and His written Word to follow until His return.

When I lived in Michigan, I would often see a certain waste management company's trucks and one of them had on the back — the BIBLE; GOD's **B**asic **I**nstructions **B**efore **L**eaving **E**arth.

The Bible contains the WORD of GOD; it is, (indeed), basic instructions before leaving earth. Use it and allow GOD to ReOrganize Your Life. Let Him order your steps in His WORD. Just ask Him to do so and He will.

> *"Look thou upon me, and be merciful unto me, as thou usest to do unto those that love thy name." "Order my steps in thy word: and let not any iniquity have dominion over me." "Deliver me from the oppression of man: so will I keep thy precepts." Psalm 119:132-134*

> *"The steps of a good man are ordered by the LORD: and he delighteth in his way." "Though he fall, he shall not be utterly cast down: for the LORD upholdeth him with his hand." Psalm 37:23-24*

As you can tell by now, that I believe in letting the written Word of GOD speak directly, at least for the most part.

The Scripture verses which follow are just a short list of Why and How to ROYL for CHRIST:

> *"For the law was given by Moses, but grace and truth came by Jesus Christ." John 1:17*

"The word which God sent unto the children of Israel, preaching peace by Jesus Christ: (he is Lord of all:)" Acts 10:36

"And they said, Believe on the Lord Jesus Christ, and thou shalt be saved, and thy house." Acts 16:31

"In the day when God shall judge the secrets of men by Jesus Christ according to my gospel." Romans 2:16

"Therefore being justified by faith, we have peace with God through our Lord Jesus Christ:" Romans 5:1

"For the wages of sin is death; but the gift of God is eternal life through Jesus Christ our Lord." Romans 6:23

"I thank my God always on your behalf, for the grace of God which is given you by Jesus Christ;" 1Corinthians 1:4

"For other foundation can no man lay than that is laid, which is Jesus Christ." 1Corinthians 3:11

"But to us there is but one God, the Father, of whom are all things, and we in him; and one Lord Jesus Christ, by whom are all things, and we by him." 1Corinthians 8:6

"But thanks be to God, which giveth us the victory through our Lord Jesus Christ." 1Corinthians 15:57

"Knowing that a man is not justified by the works of the law, but by the faith of Jesus Christ, even we have believed in Jesus Christ, that we might be justified by the faith of Christ, and not by the works of the law: for by the works of the law shall no flesh be justified." Galatians 2:16

"And to make all men see what is the fellowship of the mystery, which from the beginning of the world hath been hid in God,

who created all things by Jesus Christ:" Ephesians 3:9

"Being filled with the fruits of righteousness, which are by Jesus Christ, unto the glory and praise of God." Philippians 1:11

"For God hath not appointed us to wrath, but to obtain salvation by our Lord Jesus Christ," 1Thessalonians 5:9

"That the name of our Lord Jesus Christ may be glorified in you, and ye in him, according to the grace of our God and the Lord Jesus Christ." 2 Thessalonians 1:12

"Now our Lord Jesus Christ himself, and God, even our Father, which hath loved us, and hath given us everlasting consolation and good hope through grace," 2 Thessalonians 2:16

"But is now made manifest by the appearing of our Saviour Jesus Christ, who hath abolished death, and hath brought life and immortality to light through the gospel:" 2 Timothy 1:10

"I charge thee therefore before God, and the Lord Jesus Christ, who shall judge the quick and the dead at his appearing and his kingdom;" 2 Timothy 4:1

"By the which will we are sanctified through the offering of the body of Jesus Christ once for all." Hebrews 10:10

"Jesus Christ the same yesterday, and to day, and for ever." Hebrews 13:8

"But if we walk in the light, as he is in the light, we have fellowship one with another, and the blood of Jesus Christ his Son cleanseth us from all sin." 1 John 1:7

"My little children, these things write I unto you, that ye

sin not. And if any man sin, we have an advocate with the Father, Jesus Christ the righteous:" 1 John 2:1

"And we know that the Son of God is come, and hath given us an understanding, that we may know him that is true, and we are in him that is true, even in his Son Jesus Christ. This is the true God, and eternal life." 1 John 5:20

"For many deceivers are entered into the world, who confess not that Jesus Christ is come in the flesh. This is a deceiver and an antichrist." 2 John 1:7

"For there are certain men crept in unawares, who were before of old ordained to this condemnation, ungodly men, turning the grace of our God into lasciviousness, and denying the only Lord God, and our Lord Jesus Christ." Jude 1:4

You may be thinking, well until the last two verses you were doing good.

Of course, there are many other "hows and whys" to ROYL for CHRIST, such as in the Psalms and Proverbs. I call the Book of Proverbs "the ReOrganizer of life". The Book of Proverbs gives instructions on life. Read the Psalms and Proverbs.

However, I would be remiss, in my responsibility before GOD, if the proper warnings are not provided.

As you can see, in the two previous verses, there are important warnings or cautions since certain men have stealthily, crept in; so because of this always put your trust in GOD, not completely in man.

Do not put your confidence in man; this is where, I believe that most people go wrong.

I do not believe that I could have said that more concisely, but, let the Word of GOD say why:

"And this I say, lest any man should beguile you with enticing words." *"For though I be absent in the flesh, yet am I with you in the spirit, joying and beholding your order, and the stedfastness of your faith in Christ."*

*"As ye have therefore received Christ Jesus the Lord, so walk ye in him:" "Rooted and built up in him, and stablished in the faith, as ye have been taught, abounding therein with thanksgiving." "**Beware lest any man spoil you through philosophy and vain deceit, after the tradition of men, after the rudiments of the world, and not after Christ.**" "For in him dwelleth all the fulness of the Godhead bodily." "And **ye are complete in him**, which is the head of all principality and power:" Colossians 2:4-10 {Emphasis added}*

Again, as a caution, it is better to trust in the LORD.

"It is better to trust in the LORD than to put confidence in man." Psalm 18:8

"It is better to trust in the LORD than to put confidence in princes." Psalm 18:9

"Put not your trust in princes, nor in the son of man, in whom there is no help." Psalm 146:3

"Thus saith the LORD; Cursed be the man that trusteth in man, and maketh flesh his arm, and whose heart departeth from the LORD." Jeremiah 17:5

So, now having provided the warning and caution:

"I beseech you therefore, brethren, by the mercies of God, that ye present your bodies a living sacrifice, holy, acceptable unto God, which is your reasonable service." "And be not conformed to this world: but be ye transformed by the renewing of your mind, that ye may prove what is that good, and acceptable, and perfect, will of God." Romans 12:1-2

Do not allow yourself to be ReOrganized by the world's ways, but renew your mind by being ReOrganized in the way of the Word of GOD, which is the good and acceptable and perfect will of GOD. This is how you can be complete in ReOrganizing Your Life.

It Is Finished

JESUS CHRIST completed, accomplished or fulfilled all things that he was sent to do. And prior to Him giving His life for us, after being crucified, He said, "it is finished".

"Then Pilate therefore took Jesus, and scourged him."
"And the soldiers platted a crown of thorns, and put it on his head, and they put on him a purple robe,"
"And said, Hail, King of the Jews! and they smote him with their hands." John 19:1-3

"Then delivered he him therefore unto them to be crucified. And they took Jesus, and led him away."
"And he bearing his cross went forth into a place called the place of a skull, which is called in the Hebrew Golgotha:"
"Where they crucified him, and two other with him, on either side one, and Jesus in the midst."
"And Pilate wrote a title, and put it on the cross. And the writing was, JESUS OF NAZARETH THE KING OF THE JEWS." John 19:16-17

*"After this, Jesus knowing that **all things were now accomplished**, that the scripture might be **fulfilled**, saith, I thirst."*
*"Now there was set a vessel full of vinegar: and they filled a spunge with vinegar, and put it upon hyssop, and put it to his mouth." "When Jesus therefore had received the vinegar, he said, **It is finished**: and he bowed his head, and gave up the ghost." John 19:28-30 {Emphasis added}*

"*It is finished*. The sufferings and agonies in redeeming man are over. The work long contemplated, long promised, long expected by prophets and saints, is done. The toils in the ministry, the persecutions and mockeries, and the pangs of the garden and the cross, are ended, and man is redeemed. What a wonderful declaration was this! How full of consolation to man! And how should this dying declaration of the Saviour reach every heart and affect every soul!" [78] *Albert Barnes'; Notes On The Bible*

How should this dying declaration of our Saviour reach every heart and affect every soul?

The declaration that "it is finished" can reach any one who is willing, by taking the time to ROYL for CHRIST. That is, by receiving the WORD, the word is near you even in your mouth and in your heart. This is the word of faith in JESUS CHRIST.

> *"But what saith it? The word is nigh thee, even in thy mouth, and in thy heart: that is, the word of faith, which we preach;" "That if thou shalt confess with thy mouth the Lord Jesus, and shalt believe in thine heart that God hath raised him from the dead, thou shalt be saved." "For with the heart man believeth unto righteousness; and with the mouth confession is made unto salvation." "For the scripture saith, Whosoever believeth on him shall not be ashamed." "For there is no difference between the Jew and the Greek: for the same Lord over all is rich unto all that call upon him." "For whosoever shall call upon the name of the Lord shall be saved." Romans 10:8-13*

And then, it is a matter of going into the world under the authority of JESUS, making disciples and teaching them to observe His commandments even to the end of this world.

> *"And Jesus came and spake unto them, saying, All power is given unto me in heaven and in earth." "Go ye therefore, and teach all nations, baptizing them in the name of the Father, and of the Son, and of the Holy Ghost:" "Teaching them to observe all things whatsoever I have commanded you: and, lo, I am with you alway, even unto the end of the world. Amen." Matthew 28:18-20*

Well, this book is finished, so in closing I leave you with this, from the Book of Revelation;

"He that is unjust, let him be unjust still: and he which is filthy, let him be filthy still: and he that is righteous, let him be righteous still: and he that is holy, let him be holy still." "And, behold, I come quickly; and my reward is with me, to give every man according as his work shall be." "I am Alpha and Omega, the beginning and the end, the first and the last." "Blessed are they that do his commandments, that they may have right to the tree of life, and may enter in through the gates into the city." "For without are dogs, and sorcerers, and whoremongers, and murderers, and idolaters, and whosoever loveth and maketh a lie." "I Jesus have sent mine angel to testify unto you these things in the churches. I am the root and the offspring of David, and the bright and morning star." "And the Spirit and the bride say, Come. And let him that heareth say, Come. And let him that is athirst come. And whosoever will, let him take the water of life freely." "For I testify unto every man that heareth the words of the prophecy of this book, If any man shall add unto these things, God shall add unto him the plagues that are written in this book:" "And if any man shall take away from the words of the book of this prophecy, God shall take away his part out of the book of life, and out of the holy city, and from the things which are written in this book." "He which testifieth these things saith, Surely I come quickly. Amen. Even so, come, Lord Jesus." "The grace of our Lord Jesus Christ be with you all. Amen." Revelation 22:11-21

ReOrganize Your Life™! Finish your decision to ReOrganize Your Life™, so that you, too, can say "it is finished".

Go get it; simply, go get it.

May the grace of our LORD JESUS CHRIST bless you.

CHAPTER SEVEN

ROYL Principles ™

Seven ROYL Principles:

1. To ReOrganize Your Life, ROYL for CHRIST first.

2. To ReOrganize Your Life, die spiritually from this earthly life and be spiritually born again.

3. To ReOrganize Your Life, prepare for eternity.

4. To ReOrganize Your Life, get GOD's **B**asic **I**nstructions **B**efore **L**eaving **E**arth.

5. To ReOrganize Your Life, always put your trust in GOD, not completely in man.

6. To ReOrganize Your Life, do not allow yourself to be ReOrganized by the world's ways.

7. To ReOrganize Your Life, know that "it is finished".

ENDNOTES

Chapter One

[1] Noah Webster's 1828 Dictionary Software, Christian Technologies, Inc., Independence, MO., 1998

[2] Michael E. Gerber, *The E Myth Revisited*; New York, NY, HarperCollins Publishers, Inc., 2001, 102.

[3] James Dale Davidson & Lord William Rees-Mogg, *The Sovereign Individual*; New York, NY, Simon & Schuster, 1997, 372.

[4] Peter F. Drucker, *Management Challenges for the 21st Century*; New York, NY, HarperCollins Publishers Inc., 1999, ix.

[5] Jim Russell, *Awakening The Giant* (Grand Rapids, Michigan, Zondervan Publishing House, 1996), 24.

Chapter Two

[6] Spiros Zodhiates, *The Complete Word Study Old Testament, King James Version* (Chattanooga, TN, AMG Publishers, 1994), Lexical Aids, 2372.

[7] <u>Ibid.</u>, Lexical Aids, 2310

[8] <u>Ibid.</u>, Lexical Aids, 2318

[9] <u>Ibid.</u>, Lexical Aids, 2372

[10] <u>Ibid.</u>, Lexical Aids, 2310

[11] Noah Webster, *American Dictionary of The English Language, Noah Webster 1828* (San Francisco, CA, Foundation for American Christian Education, 1999)

[12] D. M. Lloyd-Jones, *Knowing The Times* (Carlisle, Pennsylvania, The Banner Of Truth Trust, 2001), 164

[13] Ibid., 164

[14] Noah Webster's 1828 Dictionary Software, Christian Technologies, Inc., Independence, MO., 1998

[15] The Complete Word Study Bible & Reference CD, AMG Publishers, 1997

[16] Brown, Driver, Briggs and Gesenius. "Hebrew Lexicon entry for Bohuw" "The KJV Old Testament Hebrew Lexicon"; <u>http://www.biblestudytools.net/Lexicons/Hebrew/heb.cgi?number=922&version=kjv</u>, 28 July, 2004

Chapter Three

[17] Os Guinness, *Prophetic Untimeliness; A Challenge To The Idol Of Relevance*, (Grand Rapids, MI, Baker Books, 2003), 73

[18] Noah Webster's 1828 Dictionary Software, Christian Technologies, Inc., Independence, MO., 1998

[19] Brandon Staggs, SwordSearcher® Complete Bible Suite CD 1.43, 2003: published by IdeaSoft™, Calabasas, CA www.ideasoft.com.

[20] K. B. Napier, Doctrine, Bible Theology Ministries http://www.christiandoctrine.net /doctrine/articles/article_00081_doctrine_web.htm, December1994

[21] Brandon Staggs, SwordSearcher® Complete Bible Suite CD 1.43, 2003: published by IdeaSoft™, Calabasas, CA www.ideasoft.com.

[22] N. W. Hutchings, Where Have All the Doctrines Gone?, Prophetic Observer: November 2004, Southwest Radio Church Ministries. Bethany, OK, www.swrc.com, 1997-2002

[23] Craig S. Hawkins, The Essentials of the Christian Faith, Apologetics Information Ministry, Santa Ana, CA, 1999, Rev Date: 9/5/99, http://www.apologeticsinfo.org/ outlines/essentials.html, accessed, January 19, 2005

[24] Noah Webster's 1828 Dictionary Software, Christian Technologies, Inc., Independence, MO., 1998

[25] Ibid

[26] Ibid.

[27] Os Guinness, *Prophetic Untimeliness; A Challenge To The Idol Of Relevance*; Grand Rapids, MI, Baker Books, 2003, 118

[28] Ibid.

[29] John W. Lawrence, *The Seven Laws of the Harvest*, Grand Rapids, MI; Kregel Publications; 1995, 112-113

Chapter Four

[30] Brandon Staggs, SwordSearcher® Complete Bible Suite CD 1.43, 2003: published by IdeaSoft™, Calabasas, CA www.ideasoft.com.

[31] Ibid.

[32] Ibid.

[33] Ibid.

[34] Ibid.

[35] Ibid.

[36] Noah Webster's 1828 Dictionary Software, Christian Technologies, Inc., Independence, MO., 1998

[37] Ibid.

[38] Ibid.

[39] Ibid.

[40] Brandon Staggs, SwordSearcher® Complete Bible Suite CD 1.43, 2003: published by IdeaSoft™, Calabasas, CA www.ideasoft.com.

[41] Ibid.

[42] Ibid.

[43] Ibid.

[44] Ibid.

[45] Noah Webster's 1828 Dictionary Software, Christian Technologies, Inc., Independence, MO., 1998

[46] Werner Schott, Microsoft Flight Simulator 2004, w.schott@abbts.ch, http://www.faatest.com/downloads/simchecklists/simchecklists.html, Switzerland, September 14, 2003

[47] *Making Order Out of Chaos, Edward Lorenz*;http://library.thinkquest.org/12170/history/lorenz.html, 06/11/2005 3:21pm

Chapter Five

[48] Noah Webster's 1828 Dictionary Software, Christian Technologies, Inc., Independence, MO., 1998

Chapter Six

[49] Dyson Hague. "The Doctrinal Value of the First Chapters of Genesis" in The Fundamentals Ed. by R.A. Torrey. Blue Letter Bible. 6 Oct 2003. 23 Jul 2004.
<http://www.blueletterbible.org/Comm/ fundamentals/14.html>.

[50] Noah Webster's 1828 Dictionary Software, Christian Technologies, Inc., Independence, MO., 1998

[51] Brandon Staggs, SwordSearcher®, CD ROM Version 4.7.1.3, Broken Arrow, OK, http://www.swordsearcher.com,1995-2005

[52] Ibid.

[53] Ibid.

[54] Ibid.

[55] Ibid.

[56] Ibid.

[57] Ibid.

[58] Noah Webster's 1828 Dictionary Software, Christian Technologies, Inc., Independence, MO., 1998

[59] Robert D. Johnston, *Numbers In The Bible, God's Unique Design in Biblical Numbers*; [Grand Rapids, MI, Kregel Publications, 1990]; 79

[60] Noah Webster's 1828 Dictionary Software, Christian Technologies, Inc., Independence, MO., 1998

[61] Ibid.

[62] Ibid.

[63] Ibid.

[64] Ibid.

[65] Ibid.

[66] Ibid.

[67] The Complete Word Study Bible & Reference CD, AMG Publishers, 1997

[68] Noah Webster's 1828 Dictionary Software, Christian Technologies, Inc., Independence, MO., 1998

[69] The Complete Word Study Bible & Reference CD, AMG Publishers, 1997

[70] Noah Webster's 1828 Dictionary Software, Christian Technologies, Inc., Independence, MO., 1998

[71] Ibid.

[72] Ibid.

[73] Ibid.

[74] Ibid.

[75] Brandon Staggs, SwordSearcher®, CD ROM Version 4.7.1.3, Broken Arrow, OK, http://www.swordsearcher.com, 1995-2005

Chapter Seven

[76] Noah Webster's 1828 Dictionary Software, Christian Technologies, Inc., Independence, MO., 1998

[77] Brandon Staggs, SwordSearcher®, CD ROM Version 4.7.1.3, Broken Arrow, OK, http://www.swordsearcher.com, 1995-2005

[78] Ibid.

Look For These Future Book Titles By Ray Anthony Poole:

ROYL
ReOrganize Your Life

ReOrganize Your Life-Your Doctrine

ReOrganize Your Life-Your Relationships

ReOrganize Your Life-Your Resources

ReOrganize Your Life-Your Time

www.ReOrganizeYourLife.com

CPSIA information can be obtained at www.ICGtesting.com
Printed in the USA
LVOW10s2152310815

452220LV00023B/45/P